BIBLIOTHERAPY

BOOKS TO GUIDE YOU THROUGH
EVERY CHAPTER OF LIFE

MOLLY MASTERS

HarperCollins*Publishers*

HarperCollins*Publishers*
1 London Bridge Street
London SE1 9GF

www.harpercollins.co.uk

HarperCollins*Publishers*
Macken House, 39/40 Mayor Street Upper
Dublin 1, D01 C9W8, Ireland

First published by HarperCollins*Publishers* 2024

10 9 8 7 6 5 4 3 2

A catalogue record of this book is available from the British Library

ISBN 978-0-00-858731-4

Printed and bound at PNB, Latvia

MIX
Paper | Supporting
responsible forestry
FSC™ C007454

This book is produced from independently certified FSC™ paper to ensure responsible forest management.

For more information visit: www.harpercollins.co.uk/green

For my mum, Michelle, your inspiring strength and
warmth; for my grandma for listening to me read;
and for my late grandad for encouraging me to write.

For my Harry, the love of my life, my husband,
for whom I do everything.

And for the baby I grew but did not get to meet.
I birth this book and feel joy knowing you
were there for part of the journey.

CONTENTS

INTRODUCTION

Books are balm for the soul. If you've selected this one, you probably already know this. Most avid readers have been self-medicating the hard times with comforting books, unaware that this very practice is 'bibliotherapy': the application of literature towards a therapeutic goal. As a life-long bookworm, I have, at every stage of life, turned to books to guide and support me, and found instant solace between their pages. As a young girl, curled in the corner of the library, channelling Matilda, I learned how to dream through Roald Dahl's books. I grew up, as many did, to learn about friendship and identity through the drama-filled pages of Jacqueline Wilson novels. The biographies of my favourite childhood writers led me to the classics, and before I took my final school exams, I was tearing through the Brontës and Zora Neale Hurston in the summer sun.

Returning to these books like much-loved repeated episodes of TV shows has always brought a warmth to my chest. I feel as though I've read the words so many times they are half mine and half the author's own. The experience is other-worldly, as though I'm sitting next to my younger self, reading it back with her. All this time, I did not know this experience was bibliotherapy, and maybe you did not either. You simply enjoy the feeling of a hug from the pages of a much-loved novel – you're only human, after all. Alan Bennett said it best, that, 'the best moments in reading are when you come across something – a thought, a feeling, a way of looking at things – which you had thought special and particular to you. Now here it is, set down by someone else, a person you have never met, someone even who is long dead. And it is as if a hand has come out and taken yours.'[i]

One of the most intimate gifts, I've always thought, is that of a book. I have always loved scrawling a heartfelt note on the first page for the recipient to tell them why I've plucked *this* book from the shelves and carefully wrapped it, especially for them. Those around me can probably always predict receiving a book for birthdays, Christmas and other special occasions, but I'll also forever be known for 'prescribing' books to complement and guide people through their life experiences. A copy of *Girl, Woman, Other* for my girlfriend in need of a book inspiring sisterhood and solidarity, a clothbound edition of *Little Women* for my grandma at Christmas, a copy of *Reasons to Stay Alive* for my childhood friend struggling with his mental health. Giving someone a book in this manner has always felt, to me, like the best gift of all. It's the gift of losing yourself and finding yourself anew in the wisdom of words. Books are an invitation to evolve, and Judith Butler aptly writes: 'We lose ourselves in what we read, only to return to ourselves, transformed and part of a more expansive world.'[ii]

Our world is built on diverse perspectives and lived experiences, and bibliotherapy is a powerful tool not only for self-discovery and emotional healing but also for broadening our intellectual and cultural horizons. Bibliotherapy, when approached with intention, becomes a catalyst for personal

growth and also, sometimes, for societal transformation. It encourages us as readers to venture beyond our comfort zones, embracing stories that challenge preconceived notions and expand our worldview. Through diversifying our bookshelves and reading lists, we encounter voices that have been marginalised or silenced, historically less published, or even banned. Books amplify the richness and complexity of our world, they reflect a spectrum of identities, cultures and experiences beyond our own and encourage us to cultivate empathy, compassion and a deeper appreciation for the wider world we are a part of. In short, they have the power to help us and change us in myriad ways.

All of this is why bibliotherapy is such a delightful and exciting practice to me. The idea that we can prescribe ourselves and others books *precisely* fitting to their circumstances and emotions, and feel all the better for it. It's much more than an evangelical thrusting of a bestseller at someone saying, 'I read this in one sitting, you've *got* to read it!' It is the carefully curated art of recommending the right reads for the right time. Beyond this, reading is how we understand and make sense of the world. Whether we read online, the newspaper, books, columns, poetry; it is the way we absorb life. In ever-changing and anxious times, reading gives us a great deal of power in choosing and constructing the kind of world we live in. And in turn, this enhances the person we become, because as we absorb new novels and stories, we are forever changed.

This book is an invitation to look introspectively at where you are in life – where your head is at, and what you're feeling – and allow yourself to be guided to a book that will be a perfect fit for what you need. I like to compare the feeling of DNF-ing ('Did Not Finish') a book to being rather like impulsively buying a pair of trendy shoes. Grabbing a paperback in the supermarket for a light read is often a perfectly fine way to find your next book. Everyone's been talking about this one, so why do you find yourself unable to read more than a few pages at a time before mentally checking out? It sits uncomfortably on your bedside table for weeks, then months, before you forget the plot entirely and leave it to gather dust. Much like grabbing a pair of shoes because they're on trend and on sale, but a size too small, so then inevitably getting a blister and you never wear them ever again; the book was just not the right fit for you.

Bibliotherapy is the antidote to this, and it means you'll never have to DNF a book again. You'll find the right one for you, always, and discover new authors and stories to pursue on the journey.

The practice of bibliotherapy has been around as long as storytelling itself, but the first literary mention of it was in an article written in 1916 in *The Atlantic Monthly*, 'A Literary Clinic', which described bibliotherapy as a 'new science'. The writer described: 'A book may be a stimulant or a sedative or an irritant or a soporific. The point is that it must do something to you, and you ought to know what it is. A book may be of the nature of a soothing syrup or it may be of the nature of a mustard plaster.' In short, books comfort and heal. We can trace bibliotherapy all the way back to the ancient Greeks, 'who inscribed above the entrance to a library in Thebes that this was a "healing place for the soul".'[iii] The ancient Greeks were the purveyors of using bibliotherapy by putting hospitals next to theatres so that patients could be cured by the art as much as the medicine. The benefits now are still the same, but severely underrated and less a part of our lives than it was for the Greeks – which I take issue with.

After World War One, soldiers returning home from the Front were often prescribed a course of reading. Librarians were given training on how to give books to these soldiers, and there's a heart-warming story about Jane Austen's novels being used for bibliotherapeutic purposes. Bibliotherapy went on to be used in hospitals and libraries, and has more recently been taken up by psychologists, social workers and doctors as a unique mode of therapy. Literature has been a part of therapeutic purposes since the birth of publishing, and literary research shows that cognitive bibliotherapy can help to treat the symptoms of complex mental health experiences like anxiety, depression and insomnia. Further studies show that reading novels enhances connectivity in the brain and improves brain function, and it can even work to prevent cognitive decline.

George Eliot, who allegedly overcame her grief of losing her life partner through a programme of guided reading that she undertook with a young man who went on to become her husband, believed that 'art is the nearest thing to life; it is a mode of amplifying experience and extending our contact with our fellow-men beyond the bounds of our personal lot.'[iv] For those of us who read voraciously, we already know the good that stories do for our mental health. Beyond this, reading, as Eliot expresses, makes us more empathetic, making our bibliotherapy not only an emotionally but also a socially enriching activity.

A 2011 study published in the *Annual Review of Psychology*, based on analysis of fMRI brain scans of participants, showed that when people read about an experience, they display stimulation within the same neurological regions as when they go through that experience themselves. We draw on the same brain networks when we're reading stories and when we're empathising with another person's feelings. By reading and being immersed in a narrative, we benefit more than we could ever know by living the life on the page, and bettering our own life for doing so.

What I love about bibliotherapy is the humanity in the practice. There is something so intangibly comforting about reading the words that someone else has carefully written and feeling they were written for you, but in tandem having them recommended by a real, empathetic human. That's me in this practice, hello! There have been research studies into bibliotherapy chatbots, if you can believe it, and although I am a fan of many forms of technology that advance our access, I cannot get behind the robotification of bibliotherapy. It is an intimate practice, an exchange of words at every step of the way to get to the heart of the problem and, in my opinion, must be done by a person who truly understands what that means. Connecting the literature and the human has never been better embodied than by this quote from James Baldwin: 'You think your pain and your heartbreak are unprecedented in the history of the world, but then you read… books taught me that the things that tormented me most were the very things that connected me with all the people who were alive, or who had ever been alive.'[v]

Who better to reinforce the benefit of bringing books and bibliotherapy to greater importance in our lives than the writers themselves? Each of us comes to the practice of reading, and now book therapy, with different objectives, so the following is a collective of reasons, from the writers themselves, of why you might come to books for your healing.

'TO LIVE A THOUSAND LIVES'
George R. R. Martin[vi]

How remarkable it is that we are able to tap into this unique method of living beyond the life we have. There isn't a single person on Earth who hasn't imagined what their life could look like if they lived in another time, another country, another body. Books bring us the answer, and the opportunity. Open the pages and step into the shoes, mind and soul of someone entirely different. Oscar Wilde wisely said, 'the only real people are the people who never existed'.[vii] This reminds me of the ache you can experience as a reader when you shut a book and you realise the life you've been leading within its pages and the characters you've grown to love and share it with are now over. Living within the pages of a fabulous novel can feel just as real as life itself, and such is the beauty of a well-crafted narrative.

TO 'READ BOOKS AS ONE WOULD BREATHE AIR, TO FILL UP AND LIVE'
Annie Dillard[viii]

Reading is a life-affirming act. When we are in doubt of goodness, hope or justice in the world, we can turn to literature for centuries of proof. I like to think that reading is like finding clarity on a crisp morning walk. Having been cooped up in a home of stagnant ideas, boredom and claustrophobic air, we stand up and announce, ceremoniously, that we are 'going to get some fresh air'. We are not in doubt of its healing effect. This is how I see books, as fuel for us to breathe clearer, think clearer and anchor ourselves to the promising and beautiful parts of life, humanity and what the future holds.

TO EXPERIENCE 'A UNIQUELY PORTABLE MAGIC'
Stephen King [ix]

Escapism is a healer in its own way. When we need distracting from the world around us, a brief holiday into something else, books can transport us there. We all experienced this during the pandemic, and book sales and engagement with reading worldwide rose exponentially. We all needed somewhere else to go, when we couldn't physically go anywhere. This still aids us now. According to *The Bookseller*, sales of fantasy books have risen in the last two years; for many people entering the workforce for the first time and feeling the stress of a corporate environment, fantasy has been a balm to them, a true escape into an other-worldly experience of faeries, fantasy, romance, kingdoms and magic. Connecting to an imagined world has a wonderfully calming effect.

'TO SHOW A MAN THAT THOSE ORIGINAL THOUGHTS OF HIS AREN'T VERY NEW AFTER ALL'
Abraham Lincoln [x]

Changing the decidedly masculine pronouns of this quote, books truly do offer everyone an opportunity to assess our position in the world. We are a selfish species, often focused so entirely on our own internal monologues that we can think ourselves truly alone in having a problem, a doubt or a train of thought. Books show us there are more people like us, more people wanting to make a change, more people questioning this vision for the future. We can assess our values through narratives and expand our focus beyond ourselves. After all, it was Descartes who said books give us the opportunity 'to have a conversation with the finest (people) of the past centuries'.[xi] We can read their books, absorb their words and feel less alone.

'TO TURN (OUR) BRAIN'
Louisa May Alcott

I have always been delighted by this quote from the author of *Little Women*: 'She is too fond of books, it has turned her brain.' In the not-so-distant past, many believed that literature would corrupt women, giving them a desire for a life beyond their lot. I believe, 'turning' or 'addling' our brains by reading books should be seen as a positive thing. Stimulating ourselves, our imaginations and our capacity for empathy can only ever be positive, and books provide us with an opportunity for plenty of inspiration and motivation to look beyond the lives we have imagined for ourselves, as we dare to dream bigger.

......

Bibliotherapy exists today in many different forms, but its revival is much needed in the face of mental health crises and modern burnout. I feel strongly about books and practices being accessible to all, not gilded in academia, as bibliotherapy has been. This book has been carefully curated to serve everybody, to introduce you to stories you need to read, and to bring bibliotherapy into your daily practices. Finding the right book for the right time is an art form, and books often mean different things to different people at different times in their lives. The dream is to help you curate a bookshelf containing recommendations for every mood and every chapter of life. Turn the page, dear reader, your bibliotherapy journey awaits.

WHEN I GET
THAT FEELING,
I NEED...
TEXTUAL
HEALING

Whilst I cannot sit down one on one with you to personalise the prescription (although nothing would delight me more), I can invite you to take part in a bibliotherapy consultation of your own creation by answering the questions that follow. Think of it as a private consultation. Answering these questions will guide you to the most helpful section of this book for your needs, and to a list of recommendations of books that will have the most urgent impact on your life.

At the beginning of any good bibliotherapy session is a questionnaire or investigative quiz to define what's going on with you, where you're at, and what books can help you understand and navigate life. Put simply, it's a vibe check. Choose the answer that best represents you and collect the answers so you can be guided to the chapters of the book that will speak to you best. It's a fiction prescription, if you like.

Were books an important part of your childhood?

A   Yes, I have fond memories of reading with family and friends and sharing stories.

B   Yes, I read individually a lot and it became a special interest.

C   No, not beyond educational reading.

D   I did have a good relationship with reading and returning to the practice would be healing for my inner child.

Does reading play an important role in your life now?

A   Not currently, I find it hard to focus on reading because of everything going on in my life right now.

B   I wish I had more time for it, and for my self-care in general.

C   I read infrequently, but when I do I find books help to direct me and ground me when life feels busy and complex.

D   Yes, I know reading is important for my mental health and me-time.

Do you feel confident about your purpose and authenticity in life?

A   Ish; I have a number of complicated and/or changing relationships in my life that I feel defined by.

B   I know what I want, and I want to lean into it more, but I am scared of change and need a bit of direction.

C   Yes! I am in pursuit of my goals and feel driven towards them. I welcome change.

D   Not really. I feel I need to listen more to my body and my mind, prioritise myself and my well-being more.

What change would you like to make in your life right now?

A   Navigating my relationships with confidence.

B   Affirming myself, being unapologetically and authentically me.

C   Challenging myself, and navigating the challenges I'm facing.

D   Understanding my mental health and well-being demands.

How would you define the relationships in your life? How do you show up for the important people around you?

A   I have a lot of deep, complex relationships that define my life – in romance, platonic friendships and family.

B   I am always one to motivate and hype up the people around me; I am told I'm wise, people come to me for advice and I confidently advise myself.

C   Relationships are important to me, but I can feel lonely, especially as I'm going through periods of change right now.

D   I am a people-pleaser, I give so much of myself to my relationships and work that I neglect my own needs.

What do you feel proud of in your life at the moment?

A   My relationships with others and how I show up for them and support them.

B   How much I have achieved, and my self-growth.

C   Where I have got to so far in life, excitement that my life is changing for the better.

D   My awareness and attempts to spend more time on my self-care.

What would you say is the biggest, most defining theme in your life right now? What do you want to get from book therapy to help with these situations?

A   I want to understand and improve my relationships.

B   I am seeking to better understand myself and level up my life.

C   My life is changing in a big way and I want to be able to navigate that confidently.

D   I need to spend more time on radical self-care and healing.

How is your work–life balance, or your relationship to your work?

A   My relationships and friendships are more important to me than my work, I don't define myself by my job.

B   I am ambitious and driven, but want to be more creative, authentic and confident in how I apply myself to my work.

C   I have had jobs, but I am leaning into a career or a career-defining change that feels big and scary right now.

D   I have often been known to define myself by my productivity and my work, and I know that relationship needs to change.

What role does stress play in your life? Where would you say your mental health is at right now?

A   I feel good, and I am held and well supported by friends and family.

B   I am self-sufficient, but always curious of where I can improve.

C   I am stressed and often existential about life and my purpose.

D   I am frequently stressed, and struggle with my mental health.

How inspired do you feel of late?
What role will reading play in your life?

A   I feel very led by my emotions, and I hope reading more of the right thing will help me navigate and understand them.

B   I am easily inspired by the world around me, and always open to the next opportunity for creativity and learning.

C   I feel ready to be inspired, and open to change, but I'm in a bit of a creative rut.

D   I find it hard to be inspired or motivated due to my mental health/mental load. I want reading to give me time for myself and to work through difficult times.

Answers: Your fiction prescription

Mostly A – you have been prescribed… *the novel cure*
You love hard and are deeply emotional. Your relationships – be it with friends, family or romances – are the most important thing in the world to you. Understanding them and navigating them can be a different pill entirely. I recommend you spend time with the writers who are absolute experts on the subjects of love, friendship, trust and family to enrich your life:

First Loves & Great Loves · Heartbreak · New Parents · Escapism · Grief & Loss · LGBTQIA+ Identity Self Love & Self Discovery

Mostly B – you have been prescribed… *inkspiration*
Hello, Miss Independent! You are a true free spirit and for
that I commend you. You're driven to self-improvement and
are always looking for the next piece of inspo that will make
you a more confident, courageous and creative version of
yourself. I prescribe you with reading some of the very best
books that are going to keep you on this boundless search for
a sparkling and technicolour life:

Creativity & Inspiration · Confidence & Courage
Empowerment · Escapism

Mostly C – you have been prescribed… *turning*
over a new leaf
Ch–ch–ch–ch–changes! You are going through it. Perhaps
you're moving, you're starting afresh, becoming a parent;
whichever way, your life is going to look pretty different in
6–12 months' time. You're being catapulted into change,
which is scary but also so exciting and an opportunity you
can lean into. I recommend the below chapters to guide you
through these changing times:

New Beginnings · When Adulting Begins · Your Mind
Feeling Directionless · Empowerment

Mostly D – you have been prescribed... *a paper hug*

You are seeking healing, you-time and inner peace. It's hard to find in this busy world, but books are here to calm your mind and direct you towards your wellness. Take this opportunity to be still, be with the stories and guided by the authors who can help you. They are the experts, and they have written their books especially for you. You've come to bibliotherapy at the right time, and I am confident you'll find a warm embrace waiting for you in the following chapters:

Escapism · Your Mind · Feeling Directionless

I hope this questionnaire has provided food for thought and you're ready to start your book therapy journey. Consider discussing these questions with a trusted friend, perhaps a fellow reader or your partner, and having someone there as an accountability partner for your reading journey. A book therapy book club, if you will! If you are left with more questions, you're doing it correctly, and we're ready to embark on your book therapy journey together.

A NOTE ON POETRY

One of the goals of bibliotherapy is to make a person aware of their inner feelings at a conscious level, by introducing them to literature that, it is hoped, will speak to them or their personal circumstances. I couldn't very well write a book about bibliotherapy without including the nuance of poetry therapy. This subject could be its own book entirely, but for the sake of this chapter I am focusing on how anybody feeling overwhelmed by a particular emotion can use poetry to help understand those emotions on a deeper level. For example, you could be feeling overcome with anger, fear, dread, guilt or any number of emotions that often hover over our lives with ominousness without being able to fully articulate why you feel these feelings. Arthur Lerner, in *The American Journal of Nursing*,[xii] believed that, 'For some patients, a new understanding of themselves begins when they hear the words of a poet.' This was written in 1973, a remarkable academic debut of the concept of poetry therapy.

Now I have categorised this section not simply by it being *about* poetry, but for those who go through life acutely aware that they are feeling deeply. After all, bibliotherapy is a practice that is all about connecting emotion to the page, feeling to literature. Oftentimes, people who feel deeply are those who need to connect to words as a softener for the soul, and who are – perhaps like you, lovely reader – often consumed by nostalgia, feel homesick for their childhood, think deeply about all the lives they could lead, and are incredibly moved by art. Feeling deeply can be perceived internally as a failing, an insecurity, a vulnerability that leaves a person open to the elements in our fast-moving, cutting world. However, I choose to believe that feeling deeply is a true blessing. It is an opportunity to connect with empathy on a daily basis, to not be hardened to the news or disenfranchised from hardship, to not be desensitised to the violence and hate we see all around us. Being a human makes us inseparable from feeling, and though the world may hastily tell us otherwise, feeling deeply is how we stay true to ourselves, not moulded by the 'shoulds' and 'coulds' that mould others.

In these modern times, poetry *can* be underrated. When we long for connection more than ever through our screens, endlessly tethered through apps and notifications, but seemingly more lonely than we could have imagined, poetry is a balm. However, something that has filled me with joy as both a millennial and a person who is chronically online is seeing the interplay between poetry and our online lives, in a way that I hope would shock and delight some older generations who believe that young consumers of social media are melting away their individualism in exchange for likes. There has been a remarkable flurry of poetry-dedicated pages springing up in all corners of the internet, from Instagram to TikTok. My particular favourite is 'poetryisnotaluxury' on Instagram, which takes its inspired name from activist and poet Audre Lorde. Following these pages has been balm to the soul. Indeed, when the doom-scrolling takes over, having an online feed peppered with poetry is soothing and connecting in a way that 'Stories' and 'Reels' are not. Oftentimes, a particular poem will halt me in my scrolling tracks, as though it has stopped traffic. It is an invitation to slow down, challenge the attention span and *read*. Finding a poem that resonates in this manner feels like it found *me*, even though tens of thousands of others have also liked and commented on it. Suddenly, I am not alone. This practice, after my academic study, inspired me to pick up more short collections of poetry in the bookshops, keep them on my nightstand and flick through for spontaneous soothing when I crave the connection and elegance that poetry provides. Now, I am urging you to do the same. After all, it was Adrienne Rich who perfectly summarised that 'every poem breaks a silence that had to be overcome, prismatic meanings lit by each other's light, stained by each other's shadows'.[xiii]

This also feels a fitting place to shed light on the diverse history behind bibliotherapy and poetry therapy that in my research does not get enough acknowledgement. Sadie Peterson Delaney was a luminary figure in the realm of bibliotherapy and poetry therapy, who stands as a testament to the transformative power of literature and the importance of reading diversely.

Embracing the moniker of bibliographer, Delaney transitioned from her role as a librarian to a trailblazer in the field of bibliotherapy and poetry therapy. Her passion for providing access to prescribed books made her a figure of influence in the literary landscape. Her work was particularly pronounced within the Black community, where she tirelessly championed the cause of bibliotherapy and poetry therapy. She especially emphasised her work to Black veterans by providing them with books and poetry by diverse authors and with diverse characters. Delaney saw the library as helping them in their 'upward struggle to lay aside prejudice, all sense of defeat, and to take in that which is helpful and inspiring by the means of books.' Her emphasis on aiding individuals in overcoming obstacles through stories and prose encapsulates the spirit of her bibliotherapeutic endeavours, and demonstrates a keen awareness of the therapeutic impact of books by authors who shared a cultural background.

Poetry therapy, like bibliotherapy, is taken to be a tool not a school. It is part of a much larger and wider connection of therapeutic aid. However, what is fascinating about the practice of poetry therapy is that it is well known to unlock creativity in the reader in a way they perhaps had not previously experienced. Feeling moved by the poetry they read that mirrors their personal circumstance, it catalyses creativity to write poems of their own experience. 'One reacts, not just to what is written but to what seems to hover around it unwritten',[xiv] D. R. Frampton writes of poetry, and I always find that the blank white page around a poem feels inviting to annotate, and connect uniquely to the words, an invitation to adopt your own meaning and write yourself anew. A misconception may be that writing poetry *has* to be for an audience, or with a view to being perceived as a 'poet'. Very few poets would say they habitually write to publish. They would tell you they write because it compels them: the words demand to be written and edited and written again until what preoccupies their mind is out on the page with clarity and completion. So, if you are feeling inspired after perusing some poetry online or from a collection you have picked up at a bookshop, why not give poetry writing a go? It might just give you that extra bit of clarity you need to move through your bibliotherapy journey.

1.

CONFIDENCE
& COURAGE

A common misconception when looking for a book to inspire confidence would be that it must sit in the 'feelgood self-help' section of a bookshop. I would argue that the very best reads to inspire courage feature messy, complex characters who, like us, worry about the result of their decisions but hurtle through life in search of freedom and happiness all the same. A remarkable heroine who chooses to leave a toxic marriage and finds herself in Paris (thank you, Jean Rhys), inspires far more than any 'ten-step plan to a better you' ever could.

Well-crafted narratives not only enable us to connect with the main character's transformative odyssey, but they also inspire an introspective odyssey of our own. Typically, the character in a novel follows a trajectory, resulting in an improved version of themselves. By immersing ourselves in their narrative, we are inspired to revaluate what we deem 'significant' in our own lives. In the bibliotherapy world, this practice is known as 'narrative therapy'; it's essentially the science behind why we often feel empowered and self-assured after connecting so deeply with a character who has undergone a transformation.

On a personal note, I cannot possibly explain how much my life changed when I first read Henrik Ibsen's *A Doll's House*, a play that documents Nora, an unfulfilled housewife desperate for escape from her situation in any form. To the reader, it appears she is throwing her life away – husband, children and a happy home – but looking into the historical context, this was a life Nora did not choose. She was shackled to being a homemaker, but she wanted freedom, excitement and, oh-so-shockingly, a sense of passion and desire. Watching a character evolve, take the reins and carve a new path for themselves beyond the status quo can spark the shift in our mindset we desperately need. It can gently prod us to veer off course a little, whether that translates as a move to a new city, to take a new lover or pursue a new motivation. These characters encourage us to live boldly by alleviating any apprehension linked to change, and instead we are asked to focus on how wonderful life could be if we were to take the plunge. Is there a more freeing thought?

Witnessing the journeys of self-discovery and positive (though challenging) change for complex female characters has long inspired me to be more open to change, confidence and excitement in my own life, my own story. For me, this courage and confidence usually comes from the narratives of women navigating times where their choices and freedoms were limited. Whilst I am drawn to these narratives of plucky heroines going against society's expectations of them and choosing courage and confidence, you as a reader will find similar inspiration in all the books I have recommended. I hope this affirmation will be kick-started by the narratives of these women and their Parisian escapades, and you'll be inclined to pursue your aspirations, regardless of what holds you back. With greater obstacles, their gumption and self-assuredness had to be louder, in order to create radical change towards happier and more selfish life choices, in a world that wanted them to be something different. These books, and especially their central characters, were often not well received in their time, for questioning the norm and seemingly promoting narratives of women leaving their domesticated roles in pursuit of something more. I say, what could be more inspiring to a reader in need of a dose of confidence than a protagonist challenging convention, against all odds, to create a more meaningful and fulfilling life?

GOOD MORNING, MIDNIGHT
by Jean Rhys

This book is my Roman empire, in essence – it is something I think about at least once a day! (Apparently most men think about the Roman empire at least once a day, and thus began a trend of 'what's yours?') Ever since I read this book at university, it has not left my mind, and the character of Sasha is someone I tell people about as if I'm speaking about an old friend. Reading Rhys is a truly captivating and hypnotic affair, her prose is lucid and sharp, and she writes the most fascinating psychological portraits of women in desperate situations. If you are also a writer, Jean Rhys will undoubtedly inspire you to become a better writer, with her daring narratives and mesmerising prose.

Good Morning, Midnight is the story of Sasha, a woman in 1930s Paris wandering from bar to seedy hotel and back again, after having done the same thing in London to escape her inner monologue and tormenting past. It is argued that in Sasha Rhys wrote the first female flaneur (a French term for someone – usually a man – who wanders the city streets in observation, a freedom not often afforded to women at that time). Sasha's life is desperate; she is aware of her fading youth but she still yields attention from men, she dresses well but has no money, and she mourns for an infant she lost but never told her husband about. But somewhere amidst her depression and suicidal thoughts, this stream-of-consciousness novel presents us with fragments of a whole life.

Instead of positioning this recommendation as something *filled* with confidence and courage, I would offer this up as a book of hope. Hopeful, in the way that it paints Sasha's life as something utterly despairing but pierced sharply with observational humour. Sasha has an overwhelming hatred for everything, but she also has a willingness to see the comedy, even absurdity, in the most bitter memories and humiliating encounters. It is this that brings her back from the brink. Even in the midst of her despair and frequent crying in public, Sasha retorts: 'That is the only advantage women have over men – at least they can cry.' There is so much you could say about this novel, but no words I write to convince you to read it will do justice to Rhys. To read it is to experience a fever dream – one that will be particular to you.

Good Morning, Midnight is a non-story and a complex narrative all at once; a book in which nothing and everything happens. Although we may not all have reached Sasha's point of desperation and disaffection, on dark days we can certainly relate to the absence of joy she is experiencing. Inspired by Emily Dickinson's 'Poem 382', both writers were unable to accept the place in which society so wanted to put them. Neither wished to adhere to the strict gendered roles that were expected of them, and so they turned to their writing to enact what liberty and escape could look like. It is this act of confidence and courage that makes this novel a must-read.

THE DUD AVOCADO
by Elaine Dundy

Against the backdrop of the 1950s, Sally Jay Gorce, a youthful and appealing American, finds herself in Paris, fuelled by the financial support of her uncle and an earnest desire for a vibrant sojourn. Her escapades, however, are not without their complexities. Adorning her hair in hues of pink, she traverses the city donning ensembles that could be classified as Tyrolean Peasant, Bar Girl and Dreaded Librarian. A woman who already knew the value of a vibe check.

With a vivacious spirit, she endeavours to outshine the Parisians through her audacious exploits, navigating a tapestry of cocktail parties, sexual quandaries, love affairs, disillusionments, inebriation, fiscal losses and even the misplacement of her passport (we've all been there). Sally Jay Gorce emerges as a multifaceted character, embodying both complexity and charm. Positioned as a likeable heroine, she unabashedly pursues pleasure and romantic encounters, challenging societal norms. Her authenticity, replete with imperfections, renders her a compelling and relatable protagonist. As in many of the books I recommend in this particular chapter, the setting is Paris. A cultural hub and idyllic escape of the time, many of these heroines found themselves in Paris, or yearning for it, as a city that carried the hope of change, rebellion and creativity.

Reading *The Dud Avocado*, you cannot help but be inspired by the whimsy and delightful nature of Sally Jay. She has an unreliable nature, and I admit, her dizziness and happy-go-lucky attitude that one could only have acquired by having a rich uncle bankroll their aimless trip *is* at times annoying, but to this I say, 'Who wouldn't want to be in her shoes?' A far cry from the positions of Emma Bovary (see next entry) and Sasha, this narrative was still deemed controversial in depicting a fully free woman. In a brief afterword, Elaine Dundy explains that the book is, in fact, semi-autobiographical: 'All the impulsive, outrageous things my heroine does, I did. All the sensible things she did, I made up.' It was autobiographical enough that her husband at the time threatened her with divorce if she wrote a second novel. (She did, and he did.)

The narrative's intrigue lies in Dundy's deliberate choice to prolong the storyline beyond potential concluding points. Instead of opting for an earlier resolution, she extends the tale, weaving in layers of significance, meaning and an authentic blend of joy and romance. This strategic narrative decision captivates the reader, ensuring a sustained engagement with the unfolding events and enriching the overall reading experience. The merit of *The Dud Avocado* does not hinge upon a conventional plot structure; rather, it unfolds as a helter-skelter of scenarios chronicling the escapades of a young woman revelling in her unrestrained lifestyle, savouring every moment with unabashed delight. The result is a vivacious chronicle that defies traditional literary constraints, offering readers an unconventional and whimsical journey through the protagonist's unbridled pursuit of freedom and enjoyment. You'll finish the book with a fire in your belly, on high alert to find your own moments of joy.

MADAME BOVARY
by Gustave Flaubert

The debut novel by Gustave Flaubert offers readers the mesmerising story of Emma Bovary, a woman caught between passion and convention as she strives for more than her lot. Longing for an escape from the banalities of provincial life, Emma tries everything a woman in the eighteenth century can to fill the emptiness in her life. I am a firm believer that if a book has ever been on trial or banned, it is thoroughly worth reading. This is the case for *Madame Bovary*, which public prosecutors attacked for obscenity. The resulting trial in January 1857 made the story notorious, and unforgettable. Despite numerous critics deeming this a story of a woman with broken dreams, and often a selfish housewife at that, I believe Emma's story is one of a woman with the courage to imagine a life greater than was offered by the hand she had been dealt. Whilst the liberties of women today are still hard-fought and much more progress is needed, it is invariably hard for women in the Western world to imagine the horror of living with such limited choices.

In his characteristic, beautiful prose, Flaubert describes: 'But she – her life was cold as a garret whose dormer window looks on the north, and ennui, the silent spider, was weaving its web in the darkness in every corner of her heart.'

Emma marries her husband as a means of escape, as did many women of her time, and the social elevation this gave her offered up a greater sense of freedom than what she had before. Although, in close quarters, Jane Austen was giving many readers a sense of how marriages could be for love rather than social course, unfortunately this was a fantasy, and many women in Emma Bovary's situation found themselves in marriages of convenience or arrangement. Her bursts of confidence that another life is possible for her come from books. As a domestic woman, she has very little to do after marriage, so she takes herself to reading every day. Her mother-in-law and husband conspire to stop her reading novels, as they decide that this practice is leading her astray and filling her head with fantasies. Emma is further domesticated by having a child, part of the obligation of marriage, but her desire for freedom doesn't stop here. She wishes for a son, so that he may have the liberties she lacks: 'She hoped for a son; he would be strong and dark; she would call him George; and this idea of having a male child was like an expected revenge for all her impotence in the past. A man, at least, is free; he may travel over passions and over countries, overcome obstacles, taste of the most far-away pleasures. But a woman is always hampered.'

Flaubert perfectly crafts an engaging story that transcends the centuries, documenting Emma's battles between temptation and convention, obedience and deviation. She is a complex female character if there ever was an archetype, and although she tries to reform, the more she tries to be content, the more opportunities she is met with to follow her passions. Being incredibly ahead of its time, Flaubert boldly offers insight into how jealousy and envy of the opposite sex fuels Emma's decent into chaos: 'She would have liked to strike all men, to spit in their faces, to crush them, and she walked rapidly straight on, pale, quivering, maddened, searching the empty horizon with tear-dimmed eyes, and as it were rejoicing in the hate that was choking her.' This book is so much a modern tragedy where a soul is doomed because she appreciates and battles against all that comes her way. Despite her limitations in life, Emma has an unbridled grasping to pursue her fantasies. Emma Bovary is a courageous and confident character, in her irresponsible choices that bring her closer to the happiness she wants, even if doing so she is able to attain only a glimpse of her dreams. Her story exists so that other women could strive for more.

YOUR FICTION READING LIST

Lessons in Chemistry by Bonnie Garmus
shows you how daring and embracing change can
empower your life and the lives of others

Late Bloomers by Deepa Varadarajan
demonstrates how to navigate hardship with a family

Don't Look at Me Like That by Diana Athill
provides contrasts of what love and loyalty mean to
different people and the choices they make

After Claude by Iris Owens
reveals how a change of life and heart can still be
joy filled and empowering after hardship

The Wren, The Wren by Anne Enright
reinforces to you the strength of women's resilience

Cassandra at the Wedding by Dorothy Baker
emphasises the importance of coming to
terms with the only life you have

August Blue by Deborah Levy
expands your understanding of the ways in which we seek to find
ourselves in others and recreate ourselves again and again

The Vulnerables by Sigrid Nunez
demonstrates how we bring courage to times
of uncertainty and grow through change

Fire Rush by Jacqueline Crooks
lays bare emotional honesty about love, freedom and the Black
experience, whilst portraying a powerful female protagonist
who is sure to inspire confidence

Salvage the Bones by Jesmyn Ward
shows you what protecting, nurturing and sacrificing for one's
children really means as a courageous mother

Little Women by Louisa May Alcott
empowers you with the narratives of enduring hardship
through joy and togetherness, and the choices we
make as characters of our own destiny

Three Strong Women by Marie NDiaye
reveals how ordinary women discover unimagined reserves
of strength, even as their humanity is chipped away

Daughter of Fortune by Isabel Allende
shows you how a search for love can lead us to personal freedom

...cake by Babirye Bukilwa
conveys what taking the courage to heal and move
on from generational trauma looks like

Wandering Souls by Cecile Pin
explores a tender portrait of three child refugees stuck in Lost and Found,
and their journeys through our messy, fragmented world

The Book of Night Women by Marlon James
immerses readers in the lives of enslaved women in
eighteenth-century Jamaica, portraying their resilience and rebellion

Lone Women by Victor LaValle
explores the lives of women navigating the challenges
of modern society, blending elements of fantasy and reality

I Am Not Your Perfect Mexican Daughter by Erika L. Sánchez
explores the challenges faced by a young Mexican–American girl in
reconciling cultural expectations with her own dreams and aspirations

Marriage of a Thousand Lies by S. J. Sindu
delves into the complexities of love, cultural expectations, and the pursuit
of authenticity as a Sri Lankan American woman navigates societal norms

Breasts and Eggs by Mieko Kawakami
explores the intricacies of womanhood, family, and societal
expectations in contemporary Japan

Where the Wild Ladies Are by Matsuda Aoko
depicts a collection of reimagined folktales offering a feminist
perspective, exploring the lives of women who defy societal
expectations and embrace their own agency

YOUR NON-FICTION READING LIST

Walking Through Clear Water in a Pool Painted Black by Cookie Mueller
inspires you as a memoir to the zest of living vibrant lives

Untamed by Glennon Doyle
shows you what it means to live authentically and without guilt

Here for It by R. Eric Thomas
resonates deeply and joyfully with everyone who has ever felt
pushed to the margins, struggled with self-acceptance or wished
to shine more brightly in a dark world

You Are a Badass by Jen Sincero
offers a motivational guide to encourage you to tap into your inner
potential, overcome self-doubt and live a bold, badass life

Daring Greatly by Brené Brown
explores vulnerability and courage, advocating for embracing
imperfections to live a more fulfilled and connected life

Know Your Worth by Anna Mathur
provides insights and strategies to help individuals recognise
and assert their own value in all aspects of life

The Mountain is You by Brianna Wiest
guides readers through the process of self-discovery
and personal transformation, using the metaphor of
conquering one's internal mountains

The Gifts of Imperfection by Brené Brown
encourages readers to let go of societal expectations and embrace their
authentic selves by embracing vulnerability and imperfection

The Happiness Project by Gretchen Rubin
shares the author's year-long experiment in pursuing happiness, offering
practical insights and achievable tips for a more joyful life

What We Carry by Maya Shanbhag Lang
explores the complex relationships within the author's family,
reflecting on the impact of cultural expectations and the
search for individual identity

Girl, Wash Your Face by Rachel Hollis
challenges women to break free from the lies that hold them back,
inspiring them to pursue their true, authentic selves

Year of Yes by Shonda Rimes
shares the author's transformative journey of saying
'yes' to new experiences, leading to personal growth,
empowerment and self-discovery

Good Vibes, Good Life by Vex King
explores the power of positive thinking and self-love, providing
practical advice to create a life filled with good vibes

Manifest by Roxie Nafousi
offers a guide to manifesting one's desires through
self-love, mindfulness and intentional living

Feel the Fear and Do it Anyway by Susan J. Jeffers
provides practical strategies for overcoming fear and embracing
challenges to achieve personal growth and success

Healing Is the New High by Vex King
explores holistic approaches to healing, combining spiritual wisdom,
self-care and personal development for a transformative journey

Women Living Deliciously by Florence Given
empowers women to embrace their uniqueness, challenging societal
norms and encouraging a life lived authentically and deliciously

New Methods for Women by Sharmadean Reid
explores innovative approaches for women
in various aspects of life, encouraging them to break down
barriers and define success on their terms

Black Girl, No Magic by Kimberly McIntosh
delves into the experiences of Black women in contemporary society,
challenging stereotypes and celebrating resilience

2.

when
adulting
begins

Your twenties is a pivotal decade. You leave the comfort of childhood and education, and suddenly you're supposed to know how to be an adult. As you navigate the new world in front of you like a Yellow Brick Road, you'll make mistakes and changes, celebrate milestones, learn lessons in love and mourn missed opportunities. It's an important, fundamental time to explore who you are, who you want to be and what matters most to your happiness.

When I started writing this book, this in particular felt like one of the most important chapters. It spoke to me so loudly as someone who spent so much of their twenties confused. It is such a defining decade in our lives, and so much of my purpose in writing this has been collating books that will genuinely change the way you see the world. Nothing is more imperative than expanding your horizons, pushing yourself beyond your comfort zone, and finding the voices of mentors and idols you can follow on your path to your most authentic self in your twenties (and beyond).

There is so much pressure on this small bracket of time to 'figure everything out', and it warps our perception of our twenties as having to be a hugely pressurised and fast-paced period, accelerating us towards our 'adult self'. There is so much noise around what you 'should' be doing in these years, whether it's defining your career, starting a family, travelling as a digital nomad, doing a PhD, starting a business; it's overwhelming. Not least because some of the noise is coming from ourselves – constantly comparing our (lack of) achievements to others.

Departing education and leaving behind pre-made friendship groups is usually only the beginning of the diaspora that comes with your early twenties, and it's enough to put you in a spin. I know I spent my first year after uni living alone in a new city wondering what I had done, having left everything that I knew and was comfortable with. I mused on whether I'd moved to the right place, chosen the right career path, ghosted the wrong dates, been too impatient, too impulsive, not impulsive enough, not spontaneous enough. I prefer now to think of my twenties as laying the table that I will eat at later in life. It's not the whole meal, it's the tasting menu, a chance to experiment, fail, break, mend and explore in a new-found freedom.

The first book that gave me an enormous source of comfort at this time was *The Bell Jar* by Sylvia Plath. It contains a glorious passage about the main character, Esther's life spanning in front of her like a fruiting fig tree, each fig representing a choice or path she could take. On the tree's branches are beautiful fruits: a joyful family life, an accomplished career, adventure. But Esther is bound to only choose one, and while she agonises over her decision, all the figs rot and crumble to the ground. Nearly every young person can relate to the fig tree: that horrible, suffocating feeling of indecision, the sense that every choice you make for the future means giving up on ten other choices. I felt seen reading this in my early twenties, but concerned the book would not offer up any conclusion to Esther's despair, which felt so similar to my own. However, when I reread *The Bell Jar* in my late twenties, when my life was changing dramatically (I had severe burnout, was taking a risk stepping away from some areas of my work, work I believed had defined me for many years, and I was having a crisis), I was struck by a particular section where Esther talks of her desire for a life without 'infinite security', but with 'change and excitement'. It brought me so much comfort to see the confusion, tumultuousness and lack of direction that Esther reflects back at us as readers. What I gathered from Sylvia Plath, and so many other writers I sought out at this stage of my life, was that we can and do contain multitudes, and our lives are not limited to or defined by one choice. I took a branch of hope away from the reading experience, no longer feeling paralysed by choice, instead excited by possibility.

Another form of bibliotherapy I recommend having a go at is one called 'expressive writing'. It emerges as a cathartic and transformative practice, offering solace through the act of pouring one's thoughts onto paper without inhibition or censorship. The concept of turning to a journal as a therapeutic tool has been championed by writers and scholars alike. Julia Cameron, in her seminal work *The Artist's Way*, advocates for the practice of morning pages – three pages of longhand, stream-of-consciousness writing done first thing in the morning. She emphasises the unfiltered nature of this process, noting, 'Once we get those muddy, maddening, confusing thoughts [nebulous worries, jitters and preoccupations] on the page, we face our day with clearer eyes'.[xv]

Renowned authors such as Anaïs Nin and Virginia Woolf have extolled the virtues of journaling, with Nin expressing, 'We write to taste life twice, in the moment and in retrospection,' encapsulating the therapeutic essence of capturing the intricacies of one's inner world through the written word. The freedom to articulate thoughts and emotions in a journal becomes a profound avenue for self-exploration and healing.

A way to find method through all this madness that you might also be experiencing is to turn to the people who have been there, done that. What better way to do that than to look to the shelves, and hear the stories and absorb the wisdom of some of the sage voices of authors we trust? I turned to Sylvia Plath, Dolly Alderton, bell hooks and so many others in my hours of turmoil as a young twenty-something, and they brought me out of the darkness of fuzzy-headed confusion like the voices of big sisters I never had. I hope with this chapter to create a chorus of 'big sister' voices for you to explore and hopefully resonate with, as well as explore works of great classic literature that truly stand the test of time in reflecting the lived experience of young people navigating the world alone for the first time.

NW
by Zadie Smith

The first of these literary big sisters is none other than Zadie Smith. Zadie is absolutely one of those writers who is producing classics of tomorrow, today. Smith published her debut, *White Teeth*, whilst still at university, and this has impacted her writing in a way that means she has always been writing with the immediacy and experience of the current moment, as though she is living through the times of her characters. She writes the world she sees, and in that way she becomes a comforting and inspiring voice for readers wanting the guidance of an elder sibling to walk them through each new chapter of life. Specifically, her striking novel *NW*. It takes its namesake from being set in north-west London, capturing the messiness of metropolis life for four characters – Leah, Natalie, Felix and Nathan – as they evolve to make their adult lives outside of Caldwell, the council estate they grew up on. Blending modernist, experimental prose à la James Joyce (but better) with beautiful cadence that channels the essence of each character's core through poetry, fragmentation, dialogue and prose, this book beautifully captures the chaos of London in your twenties.

Smith is consistently brilliant at contemporary social observation, at drawing attention to new and revealing speech patterns and behavioural quirks. Reading this book will make you feel like you're in the midst of a vibrant but quotidian conversation with your closest friends, navigating this new life together. It features effortlessly real characters, each defined by their new beginnings; whether it's reformed drug addiction, hustling, reinventing themselves down to their names, they come together to navigate their shared experience. I cannot promise this is an easy novel to read; it twists and turns, and fragments from one character's narrative to the next, but with a novelist as skilled and intentional as Zadie Smith, this has to be understood as a plot device. It is a way of making the reader feel as disorientated and messy as the characters themselves. Whilst this is a hard novel to read, it's even harder to put down. One of my favourite quotes to make the case for the urgency of reading this book is the following: 'Not everyone wants this conventional little life you're rowing your boat toward. I like my river of fire. And when it's time for me to go I fully intend to roll off my one-person dinghy into the flames and be consumed. I'm not afraid.'

Inspiring and unusual, *NW* is a kaleidoscope of city life and particularly the lives of four people – stark, beautiful, chaotic, brutal, electric and intense. 'I am the sole author of the dictionary that defines me,' says someone on the radio at the beginning of the novel. It raises a question mark that hangs over *NW* like a whispering ghost. *NW* was, Smith has said, her attempt at writing the first 'Black existential novel' that asks: to what extent, really, are we the 'sole authors' of our lives?

GIOVANNI'S ROOM
by James Baldwin

A book I will forever be evangelical in my recommendation of is *Giovanni's Room*. This amazing and essential book is a must-read for your twenties, or indeed any formative time of your life. Prepare to be overpowered by the richness and emotion that James Baldwin packs into each page. This book will change you, whether you like it or not. *Giovanni's Room* is a classic of Black queer literature which documents the experience of main character, David, a young American man coming to terms with his sexuality through a love affair with a barman in Paris. In a way that mirrors the human experience to its core, Baldwin's work with this novel proves how we may be the sum of our choices, but also the sum of our changes. At its core, *Giovanni's Room* is a book we can all identify with in seeing how the themes of love, guilt and inner battles with selfhood play out. It is a book about the force and fire of love, transcending all else. The following quote alone will make you want to read this book:

'And this was perhaps the first time in my life that death occurred to me as a reality. [...] But the silence of the evening, as I wandered home, had nothing to do with that storm, that far-off boy. I simply wondered about the dead because their days had ended and I did not know how I would get through mine.'

A novel that deals with so much of the human psyche and the complex emotions we feel as we grow into our most authentic selves, as well as the socially enforced expectations that bind us, *Giovanni's Room* is simply one of the most important books you can read at this formative moment in your life.

A LITTLE LIFE
by Hanya Yanagihara

Whenever I am about to speak about, or indeed write about, this book, I feel myself draw in a huge breath. It is as though I'm already predisposed to the likelihood that even mentioning my experience reading this book will take the air right out of my lungs and leave me doubled over crying on the bathroom floor. I'd like to be able to iterate that this is an overstatement, but alas, the reputation of Hanya Yanagihara's most famous book precedes itself. *A Little Life* is a book I *talk* about to everyone (or anyone who will listen), but one that I recommend for precisely the right moment in life, as it is not to be taken lightly. Reading the blurb, you'll be lulled into a false sense of security that this is a story of four college graduates finding their way in New York. But this is far from how anyone, myself included, would summarise this book's plot. If I had to give you it in a nutshell, it would be that this is a book about pain, addiction, trauma and self-loathing, and it is one you'll never recover from. It will break you for the better, consume you and change you, and you'll absolutely never be the same after reading it. (Can you see why the publisher went for a different blurb?)

It is also a book that, like life itself, blends this pain with beauty and a quiet, complex compassion that I have never read before. The characters are full, nuanced and imperfect, and the book itself *is* like 'a little life'. It is more than 700 pages of the life of Jude St Francis, and it truly feels like you're walking through decades with him. Jude is someone who can only be described as a truly broken person, wanting to be fixed. The narrative details the deep trauma he experiences and how it affects his life, and the trigger warnings (for physical and emotional abuse) start from the opening pages. However, this book, and the quotes from it whenever I come back to them, leave me feeling older, wiser, tortured but miraculously at peace with the complexity of humanity and the lives we lead. It made me experience 'sonder' more profoundly than ever before: the realisation that each random passerby is living a life as vivid and complex as your own, and that through the lens Yanagihara creates, everything seems more beautiful. One of the quotes that has stayed with me always is: 'Wasn't friendship its own miracle, the finding of another person who made the entire lonely world seem somehow less lonely?'

Having finished the last few pages of this book in the bath, I then had an existential crisis while wrapped in a towel, crying on the floor of the dusty basement bathroom of my student house. I felt like I had died 'a little death' whilst reading. Almost in a chrysalis-like sense. I felt that any reader who has gone through traumatic experiences that later affected their adult life would feel seen and almost held by this book and Jude's story. I hope that, as I felt, anyone who reads this book would consider themselves reborn, with a new way of seeing and thinking.

SALTWATER
by Jessica Andrews

This completely underrated and overlooked book is one I recommend to all my friends before they head off in a new life direction. That might be going to university, moving to a new city, navigating a new job, or just feeling like the messy middling moments of one's twenties has sent them spiralling into a quarter-life crisis. All these emotions and situations are reflected back to us readers in a truthful, raw and beautifully poetic way in Jessica Andrews' *Saltwater*.

It's a visceral and immersive novel about a young woman named Lucy, who grew up in the working-class northeast of England. Wanting to escape the fate of factories or call centres, she heads to London for university, which seems to promise her a shiny new beginning and sparkling new identity. Lucy imagines herself as the 'It Girl' she always idolised; whose life is brimming with parties, romance and fully understanding Judith Butler. However, London is not as she expected. She sacrifices so much of herself to be the 'London Lucy' she dreamed of that she loses all sense of her authentic identity, so she chooses to make a radical change and swaps the city for her dead Irish grandfather's stone cottage in a remote part of Donegal.

Jessica Andrews beautifully weaves together the tapestry of Lucy's life in a poetic first-person narrative, whilst also tackling big subjects like class, alcoholism and maternal relationships. Readers at this stage of life can relate to Lucy's craving for individualism and consequential feelings of loneliness in a big city, and her longing for connection and togetherness. I frequently describe *Saltwater* to people looking for an existential read as a book with 'no plot, just vibes'! A colloquial (not reductive) way of summarising that this book is all about its protagonist, and the beautiful slow narrative and words used, which the reader can cherish and drink up slowly like a hot tea. It is pierced with striking observations about Lucy's world, like this one: 'When I was a teenager, you would go out in your little dress and your high heels with no coat and loads of makeup. But my more middle-class friends didn't wear makeup and is that a betrayal if you start to mould yourself in this other way of dressing or pressing yourself? It can feel like a betrayal of the women you've left behind. I come from a line of immaculately turned-out women, experts in dusting makeup over their faces to conceal the tremors that ran through their lives.' Put simply, this is an essential read about a working-class girl growing up to be a woman, in the place she needs to be grounded. Her story is one that will act as an anchor for any bewildered or lost reader.

DEVOTION
by Mary Oliver

'Tell me, what is it you plan to do
With your one wild and precious life?'

It was a darling friend of mine who introduced me to the magic of Mary Oliver when I was going through a quarter-life crisis of sorts. It was the kind of 'book therapy' conversation between friends that feels unintentional but picks up the pace as you ping-pong recommendations back and forth between you that have got you through the hardest parts of life. My friend said that Mary Oliver had practically mothered her into a woman, and that these were poems that made you feel like putting on glasses for the first time when you didn't know you were seeing the world as a blur. This peaceful and life-affirming collection, *Devotion*, is poetry for even the most poetry-less among us. If you find yourself never reaching for poetry or struggling to connect with any altogether, Mary Oliver will make you feel held, and you'll find yourself abrim with emotion and feeling when absorbing her words. Single lines will stay tattooed on your brain forever, and when life is bearing down its weight on you, you'll be sure to find lightness, clarity and redirection in Mary Oliver's writing. It is poetry that doesn't feel like poetry; it's a love letter to life, and our place in nature.

YOUR FICTION READING LIST

The Group by Mary McCarthy
presents a frank depiction of friendship,
sex and women's lives that remains
relevant and relatable to this day

Careering by Daisy Buchanan
provides insight into the comparison culture
and corporate competitiveness that every young person
experiences in their entrance to the workforce

Fates and Furies by Lauren Groff
shows you how every relationship from adolescence
to adulthood has two perspectives

The Alchemist by Paulo Coelho
teaches you about the essential wisdom of listening
to our hearts, recognising opportunity

Fear of Flying by Erica Jong
reveals the complexities of female desire and the journey of
self-discovery through the lens of a daring protagonist.

Imposter Syndrome by Kathy Wang
shows you the intricate dance of ambition and authenticity in the
high-stakes world of Silicon Valley, exploring the challenges and
complexities of modern professional life

The Idiot by Elif Batuman
sets out a witty and relatable exploration of the
uncertainties and awkwardness of young adulthood, capturing the
essence of finding oneself in a world of academia and relationships

A Lonely Girl is a Dangerous Thing by Jessie Tu
reveals the unravelling complexities of a woman's
identity as she grapples with the aftermath of fame
and the search for connection

Supper Club by Lara Williams
presents a liberating and subversive tale of female rebellion,
exploring the transformative power of food and friendship
in the face of societal expectations

Open Water by Caleb Azumah Nelson
offers a poignant exploration of love, race and identity,
capturing the visceral emotions of a young couple navigating the
challenges of a contemporary urban landscape

The Female Persuasion by Meg Wolitzer
sets out a thought-provoking examination of feminism,
ambition and mentorship, unravelling the intricacies of female
relationships in the pursuit of empowerment

Beautiful World, Where Are You by Sally Rooney
conveys a nuanced exploration of love, friendship, and the
complexities of modern life, offering a reflective journey into the
interconnected lives of its characters

Sunburn by Chloe Michelle Howarth
presents an astute and tender portrayal of first love,
adolescent anxiety and the realities of growing up
in a small town where tradition holds people
tightly in its grasp

YOUR NON-FICTION READING LIST

Revolution From Within by Gloria Steinem
takes you on a transformative journey towards
self-discovery and empowerment through
the lens of a pioneering feminist

Work Won't Love You Back by Sarah Jaffe
shows you a critical examination of the labour of love,
challenging societal expectations around work and its
impact on personal fulfilment

The Defining Decade by Meg Jay
presents insightful reflections on the pivotal years of
early adulthood, urging readers to make intentional choices
that shape their future

The Success Myth by Emma Gannon
offers a debunking of societal notions of success,
encouraging a re-evaluation of personal goals and the
pursuit of authentic happiness

Buy Yourself the F*cking Lilies by Tara Schuster
presents a candid and empowering journey of self-love
and personal growth, urging readers to prioritise their
well-being and embrace the path to happiness

Wild: From Lost to Found on the Pacific Crest Trail
by Cheryl Strayed
shows you the profound changes that can unfold in life
when one embarks on a transformative journey of
self-discovery and healing

The Book of Moods by Lauren Martin
unveils a revealing exploration of generational
differences in emotional processing, highlighting
the evolving perspectives on emotions
between boomers and Millennials/Gen Z

Year of Yes by Shonda Rhimes
shows you the liberating power of embracing
new possibilities and saying 'yes' to life's opportunities

The Space Between by Michelle Andrews and Zara McDonald
offers a candid and humorous take on
navigating the complexities of modern adulthood
and the ups and downs of friendship

Educated by Tara Westover
reveals a gripping memoir of resilience
and self-education, illustrating
the transformative impact of breaking free
from a restrictive upbringing

The Panic Years by Nell Frizzell
presents an exploration of the tumultuous
phase of adulthood, offering insights into navigating
the challenges and uncertainties that come with
transitioning to the next life stage

The Good Enough Job by Simone Stolzoff
offers a compelling exploration of modern work culture
and the pursuit of meaningful careers, questioning conventional
notions of success and advocating for a more balanced
and personally fulfilling approach to professional life

3.

EMPOWERMENT

This section is ostensibly about your ever-growing sense of empowerment and the support you might need as you move through life's stages. But really, it's an excuse for me to talk to you about some life-changing reads to aid your continued feminist education. Feminist books are what sparked my career, my passion and my writing; they've become my life's work. When asked for recommendations, I could go on for hours and hours! Books about empowering women are imperative for *everyone* to read. Books play a crucial role in awakening our social consciousness. They serve as powerful tools that connect us to a range of social and political issues. It was reading the works of seminal feminist authors at university that fuelled my feminism in the first place. The initial sense of relief from seeing myself in their words was quickly replaced by anger that only those of us lucky enough to have access to higher education would come across these seminal works. This realisation sparked questions such as, 'Why is it that women should have to jump through so many hoops to be introduced to books that are essential to our history?' 'Why were these books confined to the "women's literature" shelves in bookshops, or misplaced as academic, inaccessible writing, when in fact they would ignite the fire in any woman's belly in just a few sentences?'

Audre Lorde's assertion, 'I am not free while any woman is unfree,' underscores the interconnectedness of our experiences, and the urgency of our empathy. Literature becomes a bridge, allowing us to understand and empathise with the narratives of others, particularly those whose stories have been marginalised or unheard. When we only perceive our own experience, we uphold a self-serving feminism instead of a sisterhood.

This chapter is an homage to reaching that formative point in life when questioning the world and fine-tuning your curiosities is key. Forming your own moral stance, and perceiving the world through a critical eye, is your superpower, and it is an important chapter of our lives that contributes to the makeup of who we are. If you want to reignite that fire and are in search of an understanding sisterhood to support you, I recommend starting with the following books.

A VINDICATION OF THE RIGHTS OF WOMAN
by Mary Wollstonecraft

Mary Wollstonecraft's seminal work in feminist literature provides a powerful and foundational exploration of the rights and education of women in the eighteenth century. Wollstonecraft passionately advocates for women's equality and intellectual development, challenging prevailing notions that relegated women to inferior roles in society. Her work is an essential read for anyone seeking to understand the roots of feminist thought and the ongoing struggle for women's rights.

In this groundbreaking text, Wollstonecraft contends that the lack of education for women perpetuates their subjugation and limits their potential. She argues that women, like men, possess rational minds and intellectual capacities that should be nurtured through education. Her call for equal educational opportunities for women was revolutionary for its time and laid the groundwork for subsequent feminist movements. Wollstonecraft's eloquent prose and sharp critique of societal norms make *A Vindication of the Rights of Woman* a compelling and enduring piece of feminist literature. Her words resonate across centuries, inspiring readers to reflect on the persistent struggles for gender equality and the importance of dismantling oppressive structures. Wollstonecraft's call for women's rights remains relevant today, making her work a timeless resource for feminists seeking to understand the historical context and intellectual underpinnings of their cause.

As Wollstonecraft boldly declares in her book, 'I do not wish [women] to have power over men; but over themselves.' This sentiment encapsulates the essence of her argument – an appeal for women to have autonomy and agency in shaping their destinies. *A Vindication of the Rights of Woman* remains a foundational text that challenges readers to question societal norms and advocate for the equality and empowerment of women.

A ROOM OF ONE'S OWN
by Virginia Woolf

In a world where women's voices were often muted, Virginia Woolf opens the door to a literary sanctuary in *A Room of One's Own*. Picture this: a quiet room with a sturdy lock, a comfortable chair and a writing desk bathed in the soft glow of a solitary lamp. Woolf invites feminist readers to ponder not just the physicality of such a spacc but also the profound implications it carries – an unbridled realm for women's thoughts to unfurl, unencumbered by societal expectations.

Woolf's journey into this realm begins with a contemplative stroll through the tranquil meadows of an Oxbridge college. She ingeniously uses her fictional alter ego to navigate the nuances of women's access to education, economic independence and creative expression. The often-quoted line, 'A woman must have money and a room of her own if she is to write fiction,' encapsulates Woolf's central thesis – a rallying cry for women's liberation from societal constraints.

As she meanders through the academic corridors and library shelves, Woolf unfurls a narrative tapestry that intertwines history, literature and her own eloquent musings. The book is a testament to Woolf's audacious intellect, painting a vivid picture of the creative and intellectual potential stifled by centuries of patriarchal dominance. Through her exploration of Shakespeare's hypothetical sister, Judith, Woolf illuminates the systemic barriers women faced in expressing their genius.

A Room of One's Own becomes a literary manifesto, a call to arms for women to demand more than just physical spaces – a demand for intellectual spaces, spaces for their ideas to bloom and resonate. Woolf's vibrant prose captures the essence of this quest for autonomy and creative freedom, making her work a timeless beacon for feminist readers navigating the complex landscapes of gender equality.

WOMEN, RACE & CLASS
by Angela Y. Davis

In the intricate tapestry of feminist literature, Angela Y. Davis stitches together a masterful narrative in *Women, Race & Class*, a text that feels like a conversation with a wise friend who knows the intricacies of history, feminism and social justice. Imagine sitting in a cosy corner of a library, surrounded by volumes of feminist thought, and having Davis as your guide – an erudite companion weaving together the threads of women's struggles against the intersecting forces of race, class and gender.

Davis delves deep into the intersections, deftly unravelling the complex web that has historically ensnared women of different races and classes. Her words are a call to arms, urging feminist readers to acknowledge the struggles of their sisters across various social landscapes. Through meticulous historical analysis, Davis reveals the nuanced ways in which race and class have shaped the feminist movement, offering a profound understanding of the challenges faced by women of colour.

A striking quote from Davis resonates: 'It is both humiliating and humbling to discover that a single generation after the events that constructed me as a public personality, I am remembered as a hairdo.' This poignant reflection encapsulates the book's overarching theme – the erasure of women of colour in historical narratives. Davis compels readers to confront the selective memory that often sidelines the contributions and struggles of marginalised women, urging feminists to adopt a more inclusive and intersectional lens.

Davis does not shy away from exposing the fissures within the feminist movement, challenging readers to navigate the complexities with an open heart and an informed mind. *Women, Race & Class* becomes a literary compass guiding feminists through the vast landscapes of intersectionality, nudging them to acknowledge the power dynamics within their own circles and strive for a more inclusive and equitable sisterhood. It's a compelling journey that transcends time, providing essential insights for anyone seeking a deeper understanding of feminism's intricate tapestry.

THE BLUEST EYE
by Toni Morrison

A literary masterpiece, a poignant exploration of race, class and the human experience that transcends time and resonates with readers on a profound level, *The Bluest Eye* is simply a must-read. Morrison's novel delves into the complexities of identity, beauty standards and societal expectations, offering a searing critique of racial prejudice and the corrosive impact of Eurocentric ideals.

Set against the backdrop of 1940s Ohio, the story revolves around Pecola Breedlove, a young Black girl who yearns for blue eyes and blonde hair in a society that devalues her inherent beauty. Morrison skilfully weaves together the narrative, intertwining the personal struggles of the characters with broader societal issues. The novel invites readers to confront uncomfortable truths about systemic racism and the lasting effects of societal standards of beauty.

One of the book's powerful quotes encapsulates its thematic depth: 'Along with the idea of romantic love, she was introduced to another – physical beauty. Probably the most destructive ideas in the history of human thought. Both originated in envy, thrived in insecurity and ended in disillusion.' This quote encapsulates Morrison's ability to distil complex societal issues into eloquent and thought-provoking prose.

The Bluest Eye is a vital read for those seeking diverse perspectives and a nuanced exploration of the human condition. Morrison's narrative prowess, coupled with her unflinching examination of societal ills, ensures that this novel remains a vital and transformative work in the realm of literature.

YOUR FICTION READING LIST

The Handmaid's Tale by Margaret Atwood
paints a chilling picture of a society where women are
oppressed and reproductive rights are stripped away

Parable of the Sower by Octavia E. Butler
explores a future world marked by environmental collapse and
the emergence of a new belief system

Weather by Jenny Offill
captures the anxieties of contemporary life as it weaves through
the personal and political challenges faced by the protagonist

Furies edited by Margaret Atwood
features a diverse range of voices in short stories exploring
themes related to feminism, rebellion and all the names women
are called in anger

Queenie by Candice Carty-Williams
follows the humorous and poignant journey of a young woman navigating
love, race and mental health in contemporary London

The Color Purple by Alice Walker
explores the resilience and triumph of an African American
woman in the face of adversity

The Awakening by Kate Chopin
tells the story of a woman's journey towards self-discovery and
liberation in the restrictive society of the nineteenth century

'The Yellow Wallpaper' by Charlotte Perkins Gilman
critiques the treatment of women's mental health in the nineteenth
century through the narrative of a chilling short story

How to Say Babylon by Safiya Sinclair
explores the complexities of identity, diaspora and heritage
through rich language and vivid imagery

The Women Could Fly by Megan Giddings
weaves together magical realism and contemporary issues,
providing a fresh perspective on women's stories

Mademoiselle Revolution by Zoe Sivak
follows the journey of a young woman in 1960s France as she
navigates societal expectations and discovers her own path

Red at the Bone by Jacqueline Woodson
explores the intergenerational impact of choices and aspirations,
examining themes of identity, family, and societal expectations

Stone Blind by Natalie Haynes
offers a feminist retelling of the captivating myth of Medusa

Breasts and Eggs by Mieko Kawakami
explores themes of womanhood and identity,
offering a nuanced portrayal of the female experience
in contemporary Japan

Salt Slow by Julia Armfield
presents a collection of short stories exploring the surreal
and transformative aspects of women's lives

Probably Ruby by Lisa Bird-Wilson
explores themes of identity, family and belonging,
presenting a nuanced narrative with a compelling
Native American protagonist

Nightbitch by Rachel Yoder
combines humour and social commentary as it
explores the challenges faced by a woman navigating
the expectations of motherhood

The Kitchen God's Wife by Amy Tan
unravels the complex mother–daughter relationship, exploring
themes of identity, cultural clashes and the search for self-worth

The Vegetarian by Han Kang
offers a surreal and unsettling novel that delves into themes
of identity, autonomy and societal expectations

Brown Girls by Daphne Palasi Andreades
explores the nuances of friendship and identity, offering a
coming-of-age story with diverse characters

Intimacies by Katie Kitamura
delves into the intricacies of human connections
and the complexities of intimacy

I Fear My Pain Interests You by Stephanie LaCava
explores personal pain and vulnerability
in a collection of essays or reflections

The Left Hand of Darkness by Ursula K. Le Guin
challenges conventional ideas about gender
and identity on a distant planet

Women Talking by Miriam Toews
presents a thought-provoking narrative,
exploring the voices and agency of women within
a gated community

When Women Were Dragons by Kelly Barnhill
weaves a fantastical tale, exploring themes of power,
identity and mythology

Wide Sargasso Sea by Jean Rhys
reimagines the backstory of the 'madwoman in the attic'
from Charlotte Brontë's *Jane Eyre*,
exploring themes of colonialism and identity

The Water Cure by Sophie Mackintosh
explores themes of power, control
and resistance in a dystopian setting

Red Clocks by Leni Zumas
presents a speculative narrative, addressing issues of
reproductive rights and autonomy in a near-future society

Take My Hand by Dolen Perkins-Valdez
offers up a captivating based-on-a-true-story narrative
about a Black nurse in post-segregation Alabama who blows
the whistle on a terrible wrong done to her patients

YOUR NON-FICTION READING LIST

Against White Feminism by Rafia Zakaria
critically examines the shortcomings of mainstream feminism,
challenging the exclusionary practices and lack
of intersectionality within the movement

The Second Sex by Simone de Beauvoir
explores the existentialist perspective on women's oppression,
delving into the social, psychological and historical aspects
of female existence

The Feminist Killjoy Handbook by Sara Ahmed
explores the role of the feminist who disrupts societal
norms and challenges oppressive structures, embracing the
power of being a disruptor

Feminists Don't Wear Pink (and other lies)
by Scarlett Curtis
curates a diverse collection of essays, challenging
stereotypes and showcasing the myriad ways in which
individuals engage with feminism

Constellations by Sinéad Gleeson
explores the intersections of women's bodies, health
and identity, offering a collection of personal essays

Feminism is for Everybody by bell hooks
provides an accessible and inclusive introduction
to feminism, addressing the core principles
and advocating for a more equitable society

A Renaissance of Our Own by Rachel E. Cargle
centres on the importance of Black women's contributions
to feminism and challenges the erasure of their voices in
historical narratives

Being Heumann by Judith Heumann
who shares her powerful memoir, advocating for disability rights
and recounting her journey as a pioneering activist

Everyday Sexism by Laura Bates
exposes the pervasive nature of gender-based
discrimination, drawing attention to the daily
instances of sexism and the need for societal change

Men Who Hate Women by Laura Bates
investigates the roots and manifestations
of misogyny, shedding light on the impact of toxic
masculinity on women's lives

Sister Outsider by Audre Lorde
challenges societal norms and explores the intersections
of race, gender and sexuality, offering a powerful
perspective on activism and identity

Abolition. Feminism. Now. by Angela Y. Davis, Gina Dent,
Erica Meiners and Beth Richie
advocates for the intersection of feminism
and abolition, addressing the interconnected
struggles for gender and racial justice

My Last Innocent Year by Daisy Alpert Florin
reflects on Florin's experiences growing up in
the 1960s, offering insights into the cultural shifts
and challenges faced by women

Caliban and the Witch by Silvia Federici
explores the historical persecution of women during
the witch hunts, connecting it to the rise of capitalism
and the control of female bodies

Why Women Have Better Sex Under Socialism
by Kristen Ghodsee
challenges prevailing notions about socialism and explores
its potential impact on women's lives, particularly in
the realm of intimate relationships

***Why Women Are Poorer Than Men
and What We Can Do About It*** by Annabelle Williams
investigates the economic disparities between men
and women, offering insights into the systemic issues
contributing to gender-based wealth inequality

Ejaculate Responsibly by Gabrielle Blair
addresses reproductive rights, abortion and sexual health,
and evaluates men's responsibility in these issues

The Transgender Issue by Shon Faye
delves into transgender issues, discussing identity,
rights and societal perceptions

We Can Do Better Than This edited by Amelia Abraham
features a collection of essays or articles exploring various
intersections of feminism and social justice

Everyday Utopia by Kristen Ghodsee
explores Utopian visions and their
potential impact on gender equality

Revolting Prostitutes by Juno Mac and Molly Smith
advocates for the rights of sex workers, challenging
stigmas and promoting social justice

On Our Best Behavior by Elise Loehnen
explores societal expectations and the challenges women face
in adhering to traditional standards of 'good' behaviour

Miss Major Speaks by Toshio Meronek
documents the life and activism of Miss Major
Griffin-Gracy, a transgender activist

Hood Feminism by Mikki Kendall
challenges mainstream feminism's shortcomings and
advocates for a more inclusive and intersectional approach

I Am Not Your Baby Mother by Candice Brathwaite
shares Brathwaite's experiences as a Black mother,
challenging stereotypes and discussing motherhood

White Tears/Brown Scars by Ruby Hamad
explores the intersection of race and gender,
addressing the experiences of women of colour and the
impact of white feminism

Unapologetic by Charlene A. Carruthers
discusses Black activism and empowerment,
promoting unapologetic advocacy for justice

Bad Feminist by Roxane Gay
navigates the complexities of contemporary feminism,
embracing imperfections and challenging
societal expectations

White Feminism by Koa Beck
scrutinises the historical shortcomings of mainstream
feminism, emphasising the importance of
intersectionality and inclusivity

Fix the System, Not the Women by Laura Bates
critiques systemic issues contributing to gender inequality
and advocates for structural changes

The Fire Starts This Time by Jesmyn Ward
features essays and poems that reflect on race,
justice and the ongoing struggles for equality in America

Fairest by Meredith Talusan
delves into the complexities of identity, privilege
and self-discovery, examining the intersections
of race, gender and beauty

Forgotten Women series by Zing Tsjeng
profiles overlooked and influential women in history

To My Trans Sisters by Charlie Craggs
compiles letters of advice and inspiration from trans women

The Glass Cliff by Sophie Williams
seeks to alter the discourse about women's leadership and
ultimatelyinfluencing workplace change

Disability Visibility edited by Alice Wong
amplifies the voices of disabled individuals,
offering a diverse collection of essays that
challenge stereotypes and advocate for inclusivity

Warrior Queens & Quiet Revolutionaries by Kate Mosse
introduces you to nearly 1,000 women whose
names deserve to be better known

Brown Girl Like Me by Jaspreet Kaur
educates, inspires and sparks urgent conversations for change;
essential reading for South Asian women and people with
an interest in feminism and cultural issues

It's Not About the Burqa edited by Mariam Khan
represents the voices you don't see represented
in the media – seventeen Muslim women speaking
frankly and honestly about the hijab and their faith;
love, sex and divorce; intersectional feminism; queer identity;
racism and facing a disapproving community

The Good Ally by Nova Reid
provides insights on becoming an effective ally
in the fight against racism, emphasising
the importance of education, empathy and action

What White People Can Do Next by Emma Dabiri
offers a roadmap for addressing systemic
issues and fostering genuine
allyship in the pursuit of racial justice

If They Come in the Morning by Angela Y. Davis
addresses issues of racism, activism and
the criminal justice system

Your Silence Will Not Protect You by Audre Lorde
offers powerful reflections on activism,
identity and the intersections of race, gender and sexuality

BRIT(ish) by Afua Hirsch
examines the complexities of identity and belonging
for people of colour in contemporary Britain

Diversify by June Sarpong
advocates for embracing diversity in all aspects of life,
from business to culture, for a more inclusive and equitable society

4

FIRST LOVES
& GREAT LOVES

'I blame books for my expectations of love.' How often do we, as readers, hear that exclaimed? It is true, many of us whet our appetites for romance, love stories and Mr Darcy types through fiction. The most memorable and celebrated works of literature, after all, centre on the premise of love; whether unrequited, star-cross'd, or beautifully aligned. But beyond the marriage plot, there has always been a snobbery around reading romance or love stories, which I wholeheartedly reject. Regardless of there being no one person who gets to gatekeep what literature is and is not worthwhile, or deserving of popularity or consumption, I am here to make the case for reading 'The Great Loves' as being genuinely good for us. Books make us feel incredibly deeply, we all know that; however, I was drawn to make one chapter all about love, as it is a literary genre that time and time again has been studied and proven to have profoundly positive psychological benefits to those who read it.

Truly fascinating studies using brain-imaging techniques have found that when people read emotionally charged scenes in books, their brains exhibit activity in areas associated with experiencing emotions (in the anterior cingulate cortex and the insula, for those asking). This means that our brains have the capacity to feel similar emotions whether the situation is playing out in fiction, or in our own lives! These studies show that reading fiction like this can lead to activation in brain areas responsible for processing and categorising our emotions. For example, the aforementioned anterior cingulate cortex and the insula are regions linked to empathy and emotional response, and these increase in activity during emotional scenes in fiction.

The intricate relationship between literature and the human mind involves a neuroscientific phenomenon known as mirror neurons. These neurons, active both when an action is performed and when it is observed in others, are integral to the empathic process. Within the realm of fiction, especially narratives featuring characters immersed in profound emotional experiences such as love, the activation of mirror neuron systems becomes a pivotal mechanism to allow us to feel empathy towards a character's complex emotional landscape (see earlier: me crying on the bathroom floor).

In the process of researching this book, I truly entered my scientific era. I have uncovered that research into the emotional impact of reading goes beyond the physical. Changes in heart rate, skin conductance and other physiological markers have been documented. This shows us readers that emotionally charged narratives (spicy books, I'm looking at you especially) can induce changes in the reader's physiological state, mirroring the emotions of lived experiences. This powerful duo of neurological and physiological responsiveness contributes to the feeling of being transported, and immersed, into a fictional world, and caring so deeply about the characters within it. After all, it was Jane Austen herself who said of writing romance: 'Let other pens dwell on guilt and misery. I quit such odious subjects as soon as I can, impatient to restore everybody, not greatly in fault themselves, to tolerable comfort, and to have done with all the rest.'[xvi]

Whether you are in the grapples of first love or simply curious about the romantic reads, this section will show you the full spectrum of the beauty of love. Within the pages of these powerful books, you'll see all the ways love can change us, break us, rebuild us anew and stay with us for a lifetime – even if it's just a fleeting romance – torture and never leave us, and give us a reason for being. Literature continually gives us the most memorable love stories, ones that transcend the ages; moving from the stage to the page to the screen; adapted over decades to remind us of their importance.

If you've watched the TV and film adaptions of some of the recommendations below – perhaps enraptured by the adaptation of Sally Rooney's *Normal People*, bewitched by the book-to-film versions of *Wuthering Heights*, and captivated by *Netflix*'s take on the heartbreaking *One Day* – I would absolutely urge you to return to the books. Adaptations offer up a lens of seeing the story play out, but there's nothing more enlightening than returning to the text, the author's words and intentions, and hearing those love lessons from the horse's mouth. Reading these stories for the first time, or meeting the characters you've seen on the screen through the page will give you as a reader a fresh perspective and an opportunity to see the text through your own interpretation. Rather like if *you* are the director, choosing to highlight areas of the narrative that specifically speak to you at precisely this time in your life. You get to bookmark the page, underline that quote that didn't make the script and impose your longings and love lens onto the words, and make sense of what romance means to you, from the people who truly write it and know it best.

THE SONG OF ACHILLES
by Madeline Miller

A poignant reimagining of *The Iliad*, *The Song of Achilles* is not merely distinguished by its gorgeous prose; its true essence lies in the emotional resonance that permeates every page. The heart-wrenching narrative elicits tears and an ache that lingers long after the book is closed. Madeline Miller's evocative writing is epitomised by passages such as 'I could recognize him by touch alone, by smell; I would know him blind, by the way his breaths came and his feet struck the earth. I would know him in death, at the end of the world.'

The emotional impact is profound, leaving readers heartbroken for the beloved characters, particularly Patroclus, Briseis and Achilles. The storytelling is enchanting, immersing the reader in a world where every word carries weight. Each segment of the narrative holds significance, culminating in a beautifully woven conclusion that ties all the threads together.

Noteworthy are the chapters depicting Achilles and Patroclus in Pelion with Chiron, which emerge as favourites due to the comfort found in their words and the tender love between them. The progression of their relationship is delicately portrayed, with Patroclus' unwavering love for Achilles transcending all bounds. The narrative expertly employs foreshadowing and prophecies, creating a looming sense of foreboding as the story unfolds.

The concluding chapters, however, deliver a devastating blow, leaving readers shattered and unable to shake the weight of the characters' fates. The poignant declaration, 'He is half of my soul, as the poets say,' encapsulates the profound connection and heartache that define this extraordinary tale of love and tragedy.

OPEN WATER
by Caleb Azumah Nelson

Caleb Azumah Nelson's *Open Water* emerges as a poignant exploration of love, encapsulating the complexities of a relationship that stands to hurt, remains unrequited and grapples with societal forces beyond the couple's control. The narrative unfolds as two young Black British artists, connected by shared struggles at private schools and a passion for their respective crafts, navigate the challenging terrain of love in south-east London. The novella delicately traces their tentative and tender journey into love, showcasing the nuances of a connection that appears destined yet is susceptible to the pervasive elements of fear and violence.

An aching and painful love story, *Open Water* delves into profound themes such as race and masculinity. The narrative is both intimate and introspective, beautifully written with prose that at times feels like poetry. The novella's brevity doesn't diminish its impact; instead, it enhances the potency of the storytelling. The exploration of identity, the challenges faced by young Black Londoners and the trauma of racism are artfully woven into the fabric of the narrative. The quote, 'To give desire a voice is to give it a body through which to breathe and live', encapsulates the essence of the characters' journey, highlighting the profound connection between desire, expression and existence.

Open Water pairs the idea of slow love with the yearning to be truly seen by a partner. The protagonists, a photographer and a dancer, navigate the intricacies of their relationship against the backdrop of London's racism. Their journey unfolds against shared experiences, reflecting on the racism they endured in elite private schools and the struggles of feeling unseen. The narrative embraces the beauty of passion without resorting to explicit scenes, allowing the reader to feel the depth of emotion and connection within. As the characters grapple with personal histories, scars, fears and insecurities, *Open Water* stands as an exquisite debut novella, capturing the raw essence of love in its purest form.

OPEN

coffee
pastries
good vibes

NORMAL PEOPLE
by Sally Rooney

This compelling narrative unfolds to explore the depths of a dynamic where love has the potential to inflict pain, remain unreciprocated, or exist against all odds. The story centres around Connell and Marianne, two high-school students who initially feign ignorance of each other's existence. Connell, the popular and well-adjusted soccer star, and Marianne, the proud and intensely private loner, find themselves drawn together when Connell visits Marianne's home to pick up his mother from her housekeeping job. Despite their determination to conceal their connection, an indelible bond forms between the two teenagers, setting the stage for a love story marked by secrecy and complexity.

Normal People emerges as a quiet yet profound psychological character study, portraying young, adolescent love in its most raw and authentic form. Connell and Marianne's relationship is depicted as painfully real, characterised by their flaws and imperfections that make them relatable and endearing to readers. Despite their unlikable characteristics, the reader becomes deeply invested in their journey, unable to disengage from the emotional landscape of their love story.

Set against the backdrop of high-school life, issues of class and social status add layers of complexity to Connell and Marianne's relationship. Marianne, the smart and wealthy outcast, faces social ostracisation and emotional abuse, while Connell, from a working-class background, grapples with maintaining his social status. Their secret relationship becomes a focal point of the narrative, unravelling amidst the tensions arising from societal expectations and judgments. Sally Rooney's Marxist perspective adds a nuanced layer of analysis, emphasising the incompatibility between Marianne and Connell, whose worlds are shaped by capitalism and educational divides. The lack of punctuation in the book serves as a subtle yet impactful representation of their communication barriers, highlighting the broader societal issues that hinder their connection. In a time marked by a pandemic-induced yearning for intimacy and closeness, *Normal People* resonates deeply with readers, offering solace and understanding amidst a world devoid of physical proximity and, oftentimes, love. Its soaring popularity during this period underscores its universal relevance in capturing the complexities of human connection in challenging times.

WUTHERING HEIGHTS
by Emily Brontë

A dark and haunting tale of passionate and destructive love, *Wuthering Heights* stands as a pinnacle among the great romantic novels of the nineteenth century. The intense bond between Catherine and Heathcliff forms the heart of the narrative, a love so profound that even Catherine's marriage to a wealthy suitor cannot extinguish its flame. The echoes of their intertwined destinies resonate through the narrative, with Catherine's increasing unhappiness and Heathcliff's relentless pursuit of revenge casting shadows that span generations.

As a reader, the book left me haunted and on fire, with Emily Brontë masterfully infusing a depth of anguish into her characters that elicits compassion, despite the unflattering and biased lenses through which we view them. Nowhere is this more vividly exemplified than in the characters of Heathcliff and Catherine, who bear the broken heart of *Wuthering Heights*. Brontë skilfully explores the theme of identity through the other, portraying the characters' longing to be defined beyond their contained selves. For Catherine and Heathcliff, their sense of self is intricately tied to the devotion forged in their youth, a passion that illuminates the chasm between their aspirations and reality. Catherine's confession, 'He's more myself than I am', underscores the profound truth about the human experience – the desire to be intimately known by another, to love and despise, long for and tire of each other, offering a merciful alternative to a lifetime of emptiness, silence and absence.

Wuthering Heights emerges as an epic and timeless classic, encompassing themes of obsession, greed, revenge, grief, emotional abuse, inequality and even a touch of light horror. Despite this rich tapestry, it defies the conventional notion of a typical love story. In my opinion, it is not merely a love story; rather, it is the most beautiful love story that never transpired. Within this paradox lies the tragedy and power of the narrative, tormenting and passionate, revealing love in its truest form – haunted by the ghosts of our past.

YOUR FICTION READING LIST

Emma by Jane Austen
exposes the complexities of matchmaking and self-discovery
in a comedic exploration of societal expectations

Ordinary People by Diana Evans
reveals an intimate portrayal of modern relationships
and the complexities of love and identity

The Trick to Time by Kit de Waal
presents a heartrending exploration of grief,
resilience and the passage of time

A Long Petal of the Sea by Isabel Allende
shows you a sweeping historical novel that delves into love,
exile and the resilience of the human spirit

The Age of Innocence by Edith Wharton
offers a penetrating critique of society's conventions and the
impact of societal expectations on individual desires

Romantic Comedy by Curtis Sittenfeld
offers a contemporary exploration of love and relationships,
infused with humour and wit

Violeta by Isabel Allende
takes you on a captivating journey of self-discovery, love and
resilience set against the backdrop of historical events

Delta of Venus by Anaïs Nin
shows you a sensuous collection of erotic stories exploring
the complexities of desire and intimacy

Seven Days in June by Tia Williams
introduces you to a passionate and emotionally charged
love story between two writers

When We Were Birds by Ayanna Lloyd Banwo
presents a poetic exploration of love, loss and the
interconnectedness of humanity

Beautiful World, Where Are You by Sally Rooney
provides a thought-provoking examination of friendship,
love and the pursuit of purpose in a contemporary world

Call Me by Your Name by André Aciman
reveals a poignant and beautifully rendered tale of
first love and self-discovery

Talking at Night by Claire Daverley
shares an evocative exploration of love, loss and the
transformative power of connection

Heartburn by Nora Ephron
offers a humorous and insightful narrative about love,
betrayal and resilience

In Memoriam by Alice Winn
conveys a moving exploration of grief, memory and the enduring
impact of the loss of love

I Capture the Castle by Dodie Smith
sets out a coming-of-age story that beautifully captures the
nuances of love and family dynamics

Five Tuesdays in Winter by Lily King
offers a poignant exploration of love, loss and second chances

Young Mungo by Douglas Stuart
reveals a powerful narrative of love, survival and resilience
in the gritty urban landscape of Glasgow

Devotion by Hannah Kent
sets forth a haunting exploration of love, sacrifice and the
supernatural in nineteenth-century Ireland

Marvellous Light by Freya Marske
presents a delightful blend of romance and fantasy
in a magical Victorian setting

Love in Colour by Bolu Babalola
introduces a collection of reimagined love stories from mythology
and folklore, exploring diverse narratives

Noughts & Crosses by Malorie Blackman
offers a compelling tale of love and societal upheaval in
a world divided by racial hierarchy

Pride and Prejudice by Jane Austen
conveys a timeless exploration of love,
class and societal expectations

YOUR NON-FICTION READING LIST

The Course of Love by Alain de Botton
presents a realistic and insightful exploration of love,
relationships and the challenges of long-term commitment

Atlas of the Heart by Brené Brown
shares a compassionate guide to understanding emotions,
fostering connection and embracing vulnerability in the realm of love

The Autobiography of Alice B. Toklas by Gertrude Stein
offers a unique perspective on love, art and the Bohemian
lifestyle through the lens of Gertrude Stein's partner

Conversations on Love by Natasha Lunn
provides a diverse collection of personal stories that
illuminate the multifaceted nature of love and relationships

How to Love a Jamaican by Alexia Arthurs
gives a compelling exploration of love, identity and the complex
interplay between Jamaican culture and diaspora

All About Love by bell hooks
presents a profound analysis of love as a transformative and radical force,
examining its intersections with race, class and gender

The Mathematics of Love by Hannah Fry
provides a striking take on attraction and romance

5.

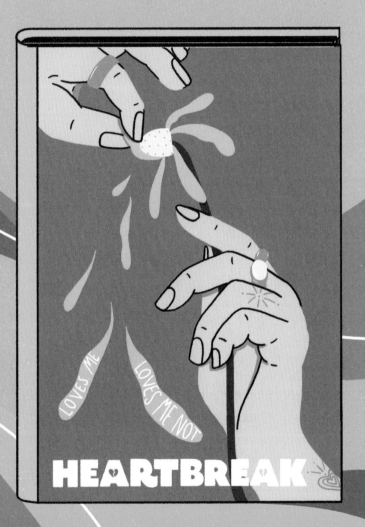

It is a truth universally acknowledged that everyone has, at some point in their life, been in a relationship that they envisaged ending like Jane Eyre's '*Reader, I married him.*' Books show us the myriad ways one can love and be loved. Many bibliophiles fill their formative years with romanticised versions of the relationships living in their heads, informed by the stories they fell in love with. But inevitably, life does not follow a *Bridgerton*-esque marriage plot, and our relationships can start to feel a bit more complicated, à la Connell and Marianne of *Normal People*. With the vulnerability of love and opening ourselves up to it, comes the potential for searing heartbreak. The kind this chapter will hope to remedy is the kind that embalms you, where every waking moment is spent feeling the emotions anew, like a tightly bound swaddle or chrysalis, until the only way to tear through the despair is to be reborn from the experience and become someone new.

Upon leaving any relationship, we are never truly the same. This can be said for platonic friendships that end abruptly, leaving us mourning, as well as romantic experiences, however long or short. We do not just lose a person and a presence, a constant in our life, we also lose the person that we were when we were with them. That in itself is an intense kind of heartbreak. It destabilises you, it can leave you feeling almost child-like in your new-found state of vulnerability, but please know that if you find yourself wailing uncontrollably on the kitchen floor, in the supermarket, at a birthday party, listening to music, looking in the mirror, that this is all part of the process and you are by no means alone.

My desire in writing this book has been to provide the kind of comfort one gets from walking into a still, antique-scented bookshop and asking a friendly bookseller stacking the shelves for a recommendation. Whilst navigating the feelings of a breakup, everyone seeks comfort, and escape. Whether your relationship ended badly or amicably, it hurts all the same. You are haunted by the conversations you had, the emotions you felt and, ultimately, the decisions you made. Your mind is full of busy thoughts, and no matter how many conversations you have with friends and loved ones, the silence when you close your bedroom door can be deafening.

It's in these early moments following The End, when you are 'feeling all the feels', staring into the void or when doom scrolling through your phone isn't giving you what you need, that books truly come into their own. When it comes to matters of the heart, books show us what we do and don't want, what we can be, how to reshape ourselves, how to reinvent ourselves outside of who we had become in a relationship (which is often moulded to that other person), and how to ultimately be more authentic. The best books allow us to escape our own narratives, offer up relatable protagonists we can see ourselves within, but they also allow us to process what's going on as we are quietly (minus the supermarket wailing) going through it ourselves.

When love is getting you down and you need comfort, relief and guidance to help you rebuild yourself, I recommended turning to the following books with a highlighter pen or notebook at the ready, so you can mark out the passages that speak to you and return to them in your times of need. Whether you're pre-, mid- or post breakup, or just asking questions about the relationship you're currently in or want to be in in the future, I hope these book recommendations will serve you on your journey.

UNTAMED
by Glennon Doyle

This book gave me a reading experience akin to a therapy session and, at the same time, a coffee with a beloved friend. Part inspiration, part memoir, *Untamed* explores the joy and peace we discover when we stop striving to meet the expectations of the world, and instead listen to and trust our inner voice. Glennon herself documents the powerful moment of realisation that she had been such a diligent and devoted mother she was beginning to die for her children, denying her sexuality and vision for her life, which is challenged when she meets the love of her life at a conference. Turning her life upside down to pursue her happiness and set an example for her children, *Untamed* shows us how to be brave. And, as Glennon insists, 'The braver we are, the luckier we get.'

It is a book that challenges how women are so often taught to be; that we must sacrifice pieces of ourselves, our comfort, our standards, for the sake of our relationships; a gentle but cutting compromise. We sculpt ourselves to become a version of a woman someone else will accept (something Holly Bourne's novel *Pretending* navigates so wonderfully, too), until we no longer recognise the person we see in the mirror.

When I started reading *Untamed*, I coloured the passages that felt relatable, teachable and important to me; until I realised whole pages were now lemon-yellow. Instead, I used the back of the book to make lists, ask myself questions and make observations about the gentle compromises and discomforts in my own life, and I would invite you, reader, to do the same.

This cathartic book is one I have gifted over and over, one I invite everyone to read to carve out their route to unapologetic authenticity in a world that has taught them otherwise. Of all the highlighted pages in my copy, there is one passage in particular that empowered me to make the necessary changes to my life.

Doyle speaks about how there is a life out there waiting for you, one that you have imagined and longed for, but in order to reach it, 'Only you can bring it forth, and it will cost you EVERYTHING.'

PRETENDING
by Holly Bourne

Another book that will guide and help you to reconcile and make sense of your feelings is *Pretending*. It follows protagonist April as she assumes the identity of flirtatious and happy-go-lucky figment of her imagination, Gretel. Following years of being unlucky in love, and experiences of sexual assault, April takes it upon herself to become the epitome of What Men Want. She becomes the Manic Pixie Dream Girl, and the reader is taken on a journey that illuminates all the ways we try to be someone we're not for someone else.

Beyond the experiment April constructs for herself, this book sheds so much light on being authentic, trusting others and working through our traumas in the name of our future happiness. It shows what singleness can mean, and who you can become when you're not under the thumb of a bad relationship. Whilst you are in the swells of finding yourself again, watching April undergoing her guise as Gretel may highlight the ways in which we can lose ourselves, and how we can go about piecing those parts of ourselves back together. You might (as I did) dye your hair pink after years of conforming to the brown your ex preferred. You might redecorate your space so it feels more like yours and yours alone. You might unapologetically start listening to the music you like and pick up old hobbies you had unwittingly suppressed.

Holly Bourne's book will show you how to mourn for the person you have lost, but also to love the space that they have made for your life to continue in a more authentic way. It will bring you strength and help you to envisage the you that you want to be.

THE WOMAN DESTROYED
by Simone de Beauvoir

In Simone de Beauvoir's *The Woman Destroyed*, the reader is given a front-row theatre seat to the turbulent emotional landscapes of three women, each grappling with unexpected crises beyond the bloom of youth. This literary triptych serves not merely as a mirror reflecting personal heartbreak but as a profound social observation that resonates with the complexities of women's emotional worlds. Published in 1967, the novel stands as a testament to de Beauvoir's brilliance in capturing the enraging, powerful and devastating dimensions of human emotion, delivering a narrative that is both exquisitely personal and universally poignant.

At its core, *The Woman Destroyed* challenges the societal constructs that often tether a woman's happiness to conventional ideals: marriage, children and love. De Beauvoir boldly asserts that these supposed yearnings may not be the conduits to true fulfilment but, rather, can erode a woman's identity when she is reduced to predefined roles.

In an era when such sentiments were radical, de Beauvoir courageously delves into the depths of her characters' experiences, unravelling the threads of their lives and exposing the fragility of societal expectations.

The novel unfolds as a poignant journey from security to crisis, spotlighting the transformative power of heartbreak. Each protagonist, initially secure and self-confident, undergoes a profound metamorphosis, ending up in a space seemingly unrecoverable from their past lives. The emotional resonance of the narrative is both a challenge and a gift; while it may be difficult to read the detailed descriptions of their heartaches at this time, it also provides one of the most authentic portrayals of human emotion. Through the characters' struggles, the reader is invited not just to witness their misery but to empathise, to share in their hopes, dreams, hopelessness and heartache. *The Woman Destroyed* becomes a poignant celebration of womanhood in all its complex, multifaceted beauty, a mirror held up to the challenges, triumphs and resilience woven into the fabric of the female experience.

THE DAYS OF ABANDONMENT
by Elena Ferrante

Embarking on Elena Ferrante's *The Days of Abandonment* is akin to stepping into the turbulent whirlpool of heartbreak – a narrative that beckons those navigating romantic challenges or grappling with the aftermath of abandonment. The book's gripping tale unravels the devastating emptiness that envelops Olga, the protagonist, after her husband abandons her, leaving her alone to care for their two children and the dog. As the walls of their high-rise apartment seemingly close in, Olga confronts her ghosts, grapples with the potential loss of her identity, and faces the haunting realisation that life may never revert to normal.

Ferrante crafts a literary mosaic that delves into the psyche of heartbreak, using Olga's story as a vessel to explore the intricate layers of emotional unravelling. Olga's introspection takes the form of letters to her estranged husband, penned with an intensity fuelled by the desperation of abandonment. These unsent missives become both a cathartic release and a haunting reminder of the fracture within her world. The narrative unfolds as a harrowing examination of hope, identity and the irrevocable changes that accompany the dissolution of a long-term relationship.

The novel's atmosphere is a force unto itself. Ferrante weaves an intricate tapestry that mirrors the emotional tumult within Olga's heart, capturing the reader in the undertow of her temporary insanity. The prose becomes a vessel for the darkness, a medium through which the vertigo of despair, the depths of anguish and the absence of light are keenly felt. The book plays with time, probes the psyche and dissects memory, skilfully narrating the accelerating breakdown of a woman's psychological and physical well-being. In its essence, *The Days of Abandonment* is an unflinching exploration of the complexities of heartbreak, a literary mirror held up to the shattered pieces of love, loss and the inexorable journey towards self-discovery.

HEARTBURN
by Nora Ephron

Amidst the symphony of heartbreak, Nora Ephron's *Heartburn* emerges as a delectable dish served with a generous helping of wit, candour and culinary delights. As readers delve into the narrative, they find themselves entangled in the tumultuous world of Rachel Samstat, a woman whose life is turned upside down when she discovers her husband's infidelity seven months into her pregnancy. Mark's betrayal casts a shadow over Rachel's world, yet amidst the wreckage of her marriage, she navigates the turbulent waters of heartbreak with a blend of neuroticism, insecurity and humour.

Ephron masterfully crafts a narrative that transcends the boundaries of fiction, drawing heavily from her own experiences to breathe life into Rachel's character. The novel's autobiographical essence infuses every page with authenticity, inviting readers to explore the raw emotions and complexities that accompany betrayal and shattered trust. Through Rachel's lens, the story unfolds as a poignant exploration of relationships, infidelity and the fragility of love – a journey marked by moments of laughter, tears and culinary escapades.

What sets *Heartburn* apart is Ephron's unparalleled ability to infuse even the darkest moments with humour and levity. As Rachel grapples with the devastation of her husband's affair, she finds solace – and occasional respite – in the world of cooking, offering readers a tantalising array of recipes amidst the chaos of her unravelling marriage. Through Ephron's razor-sharp wit and irrepressible humour, the novel transforms into a sinfully delicious concoction – a literary feast that nourishes the soul and tickles the funny bone, even in the face of heartbreak.

In *Heartburn*, Ephron masterfully blends the bitter with the sweet, crafting a narrative that celebrates the resilience of the human spirit in the face of betrayal and loss. As readers journey alongside Rachel, they discover that amidst the wreckage of shattered dreams, there exists the possibility of healing, redemption and the rediscovery of self. An offering of hope at a time when you feel so hopeless. Through laughter and tears, recipes and revelations, *Heartburn* emerges as a comforting companion for those navigating the labyrinth of romantic challenges and broken hearts, offering solace, solidarity and the reminder that even amidst the darkest nights, joy and laughter can still be found.

YOUR FICTION READING LIST

Normal People by Sally Rooney
will make you feel all the feels

Everything I Know About Love by Dolly Alderton
shows you a true and relatable account of what it's
like to live and love in your twenties

Ghosts by Dolly Alderton
will make you laugh and cry at the realities of online dating

The Pisces by Melissa Broder
weaves a tale of love, desire and transformation, exploring the
complexities of human connection and the depths of the emotional sea

Eileen by Ottessa Moshfegh
crafts a psychological thriller, delving into the dark corners
of the protagonist's mind as she navigates a life of
isolation and romantic obsession

Good Material by Dolly Alderton
explores the complexities of modern relationships, offering a witty and
insightful take on love, friendship and the pursuit of happiness

Diary of a Void by Emi Yagi
offers up a surreal and wryly humorous cultural critique,
a landmark in feminist world literature

Green Dot by Madeleine Gray
offers readers an irresistible and messy love story about the
terrible allure of wanting something that promises nothing

Black Butterflies by Priscilla Morris
weaves a narrative of love, loss and resilience set against the
backdrop of post-colonial Jamaica

YOUR NON-FICTION READING LIST

How to Love by Thich Nhat Hanh
offers advice, practices and food for thought from a Zen Masteron
our most universal emotion

When Things Fall Apart by Pema Chodron
offers profound insights on navigating life's challenges, drawing on
Buddhist wisdom to guide readers through difficult times

The Rules Do Not Apply by Ariel Levy
shares a candid memoir, reflecting on her personal journey, breaking
societal norms and navigating the unpredictability of life

A Return to Love by Marianne Williamson
explores the transformative power of love, offering spiritual
reflections and practical guidance for embracing love
as a guiding force in life

Be Not Afraid of Love by Mimi Zhu
delves into the complexities of love, fear, intimacy and connection,
offering lessons and reflections on building meaningful relationships

Block, Delete, Move On by LalalaLetMeExplain
provides insights and advice on moving forward from relationships,
offering a modern perspective on love and self-discovery

All About Love by bell hooks
explores the multifaceted nature of love, discussing love's role in
personal and societal transformation and offering a critical
analysis of its various forms

Unattached by Angelica Malin
explores the concept of being unattached, offering insights
and reflections on navigating life and relationships with a sense of
independence and freedom

Notes on Heartbreak by Annie Lord
shares reflections on navigating heartbreak, offering a personal and
introspective exploration of the emotional journey through difficult times

I Wish I Knew This Earlier by Toni Tone
shares personal insights and lessons, providing practical advice
on relationships, self-discovery and personal growth

Milk and Honey by Rupi Kaur
presents a collection of poetry, exploring themes of love, healing and
empowerment with a focus on raw and emotional expression

The Breakup Monologues by Rosie Wilby
embarks on a quest to investigate, understand
and conquer the psychology of heartbreak

Tiny Beautiful Things by Cheryl Strayed
offers compassionate and wise advice, drawing on her experiences
as an advice columnist to provide guidance on love, loss and life

Communion by bell hooks
explores the female search for love, providing a feminist perspective on
love, relationships and the pursuit of emotional fulfilment

Why Did You Stay? by Rebecca Humphries
shares her personal journey, offering reflections on love,
resilience and the process of rebuilding after betrayal

Conversations on Love by Natasha Lunn
engages in meaningful conversations on love,
offering diverse perspectives and insights from individuals
sharing their personal experiences with love

6.

self-love &
self-discovery

It was the author Gabriel García Márquez who once said that everyone has three lives. The first, the public life we show the world; the second, our private life behind closed doors; and the third a secret life, which is the world of our minds. For many of us, the latter is where questions and thoughts about sex, our relationship with our bodies, our desires, etc. tend to remain until we grow in confidence or experience, and confide in a friend. As a result, books typically provide a quiet and private place to first explore these questions. They give us the headspace to unpick our insecurities and give us the confidence to eventually bring these topics up in what Márquez would call our 'first lives'. You may have, for example, found yourself saying something to a friend like, 'I read this really interesting book on XYZ', just dying to get a conversation off the ground about how they feel about anything from non-monogamy to body dysmorphia, sexual fantasies to menstrual cycles. I specifically remember the realisation about how the school system had failed to teach me anything about my menstrual cycle. It was the words of women writers, not my biology teacher, who eventually told me the truth I needed to hear.

An author boldly taking pen to paper, tackling a topic seen as 'taboo', gives the reader an olive branch to more progressive conversations and self-confidence. Books challenge societal expectations of what should be deemed 'embarrassing', and allow people to explore themselves before they confront the rest of society.

I was one such person who felt I had no idea what was going on inside my body. I found I wasn't alone when I spoke to other cis women and non-binary people who felt that when it came to sex, our school teachers had simply focused on the dangers, but nothing else useful on the topic. Self-education filled the gaps, in the form of books like *Angus, Thongs and Full-Frontal Snogging*, and as we got older, non-fiction titles like *Period* by Emma Barnett. It was a blend of fascination and frustration to be learning about my body and the cycles it experienced in such depth, plugging the gaps in my knowledge about ovulation, cortisol surges and the pain women endure silently. It felt like by starting us off with a curriculum so sparse and focused on what our bodies could do for others, we were already being told our understanding, our pain, our questions, were not important.

To this day, some of the most commonly asked questions I receive on my book therapy podcast are about self-exploration and discovery of bodies, sexuality and curiosity. Part of the true joy of having this connection with readers through bibliotherapy is being able to point them in the direction of books that have already helped thousands of readers to answer the same questions and make them feel seen and more connected to their sense of self.

We have also seen enormous surges in the romance and romantasy book trends via new mediums like BookTok (aka TikTok). As with the typical book snobbery that seems to accompany any 'critique' of women's work or readership, there are many who denounce it as legitimate literature. Dismissing this as nothing more than veiled misogyny, my exhilaration with seeing more and more readers discover these books, recommend these books, and *write* these books lies in the veritable pick and mix we now have of mainstream, engaging, *public* erotica that teaches people about relationships to others and their bodies in a way that was not acceptable all that long ago. For many coming to these genres afresh, they may ask why people are drawn to these books. When they are not cult classics or literary award nominees, why are they selling so quickly, and why do people go crazy for them? If we return to the case for these books being a quiet and private place to explore one's sexuality and visions of romance, it's proof that such books offer up an escape, as all good books do, and affirmation. It is through affirming their own feelings, visions, fantasies even, that readers are able to undergo incredible leaps in self-development; seeing themselves reflected back in the characters, scenarios and the sex scenes in these books that allow them to get in touch with their own sexuality. A quick reminder that not that long ago women were *denounced* for this, emphasises to us precisely why these books are an important part of our reading culture now; specifically allowing women and marginalised readers to access their sexuality and curiosity in a safe way.

The way that this kind of book therapy interplays with reality is fascinating. Representation and identification/relation go hand in hand, and the theory is there to prove it.

Essential understanding is that when we see a character we identify with engage in a sex scene we find desirable, we can access it and relate to it through the Imagination Spectrum. This theory started with an illustration that covers the Five stages of Imagination. Number 1 shows an empty head, someone who hears the word 'apple' and cannot conjure anything beyond the word 'apple'. Number 5 shows a hyper-realistic apple in the head, the imaginer can see it clearly in their mind. Most people fit into around 3 or 4, especially readers, who can imagine characters, worlds, scenarios, as if they were living the life themselves. Where a person would be at Number 1 this is known as aphantasia, or image-free thinking. It affects between 2 and 5 per cent of the world's population. This means that for even the most casual reader, imagination allows us to develop further along the Spectrum, and our connection with the books we read deepens. Whatever books we read, imagining them can be as deep as *living* them, and it affirms us.

MILK FED
by Melissa Broder

What appears to be a tantalising journey into self-discovery, sexuality and body exploration is wrapped in a scathingly funny narrative that explores the intersections of food, sex and spirituality. At its core, the story revolves around Rachel, a twenty-four-year-old lapsed Jew whose devotion to calorie restriction serves as her personal religion, offering a semblance of existential control amidst the chaos of her life in Los Angeles. As she embarks on a ninety-day communication detox from her mother, Rachel's meticulously curated world begins to unravel, paving the way for an encounter with Miriam, a zaftig, Orthodox Jewish woman whose presence ignites a transformative journey marked by mirrors, mysticism and the luscious sweetness of milk and honey.

The book's decadence and overindulgence in matters of sex mirror the protagonist's gluttonous relationships, offering a window into Rachel's struggles with repressed sexuality, body image and maternal influence. Broder's narrative explores the intricate web of desire and lack that defines the experience of womanhood, reflecting on the pervasive hunger for fulfilment amidst societal expectations and personal demons. Through Rachel's introspective journey, readers are invited to confront their own fears of loss of control and the erotically charged prospect of surrendering to one's deepest desires.

With a millennial and self-aware narrative voice, *Milk Fed* navigates the darkly comic terrain of modern existence, blending wit with introspection as it delves into themes of identity, longing and the pursuit of satiation. To be a woman is to hunger, this book screams, echoing the novel's exploration of the hunger that defines the experience of growing up as a girl – desire and lack, intertwined and inseparable. The narrative not only embraces the weird and witty but also delves into the profound fear of losing control, a sentiment that resonates especially with women. As Rachel grapples with her tangled emotions and desires, the story challenges conventional notions of self-denial and invites readers to consider the liberating potential of embracing one's hunger until it is fully appeased. In its exploration of the complexities of womanhood and the quest for authenticity, *Milk Fed* emerges as a compelling read for those seeking a journey of self-discovery, unapologetic exploration and the courage to confront the depths of their own desires.

BE NOT AFRAID OF LOVE
by Mimi Zhu

This is a transformative collection of interconnected essays and affirmations that follows Zhu's path towards embodying and re-learning love after surviving abuse. Zhu, a queer Chinese Australian writer and artist, delves into the many intersections of love and fear, offering a testament to the strength and adaptability inherent in all of us.

Zhu details the immense work and self-reflection required for their own healing, opening up in a meditative and accessible style. Their writing is informed by a wealth of feminist texts, drawing on the insights of bell hooks, Audre

Lorde, Ling Ma, Thich Nhat Hanh and Mia Mingus. The book emphasises the importance of not conflating passion with healthy communication, the value of prioritising friendships and alternative forms of community over romance, and the necessity of mindfulness and being present in the quiet and beautiful moments in life. Likened to the comforting experience of a tender sleepover, where deep secrets of the universe are shared. Zhu's exploration of love and healing invites readers to lean into love with softness, making *Be Not Afraid of Love* not just a guide but a companion for those seeking to reconnect with their own capacity for love and connection.

YOUR FICTION READING LIST

Lady Chatterley's Lover by D. H. Lawrence
unfolds a story of rebellion against societal norms
and class distinctions, exploring themes of personal
liberation and intimate connection

The Secret Lives of Church Ladies by Deesha Philyaw
offers an intimate portrayal of Black women
navigating faith, desire and personal autonomy,
challenging traditional expectations

Fingersmith by Sarah Waters
weaves a gripping narrative set in Victorian England,
challenging societal norms and expectations, and revealing
unexpected twists in the characters' paths

Fear of Flying by Erica Jong
follows a bold and liberating journey where the protagonist
confronts societal expectations and embraces her desires,
navigating the complexities of relationships

The Awakening by Kate Chopin
tells a poignant story of autonomy and societal constraints,
where the protagonist seeks personal liberation and
challenges conventional expectations

Insatiable by Daisy Buchanan
presents a candid and humorous exploration of modern life, touching
on desires, relationships and the quest for personal fulfilment

Luster by Raven Leilani
explores relationships, race and identity in a bold
and contemporary narrative, providing a nuanced portrayal
of personal growth and discovery

Little Scratch by Rebecca Watson
delves into introspective reflections in the digital age,
offering an innovative exploration of modern life
and personal identity

A Feather on the Breath of God by Sigrid Nunez
offers a delicate narrative influenced by cultural and familial
backgrounds, exploring themes of self-discovery and personal growth

Acts of Service by Lillian Fishman
provides an intimate exploration of desires
and societal expectations, delving into personal struggles
and moments of revelation

Her Body and Other Parties by Carmen Maria Machado
delivers inventive and thought-provoking narratives, exploring various
aspects of personal experiences and self-discovery

Vladimir by Julia May Jonas
challenges traditional norms in a contemporary
and edgy exploration, offering a unique perspective on
modern relationships and identity

Three Women by Lisa Taddeo
investigates the lives of three women with distinct
experiences, providing an in-depth exploration of desires,
relationships and personal narratives

Poor Little Sick Girls by Ione Gamble
presents a collection of essays offering raw and honest
reflections on modern life, touching on diverse aspects
of personal experiences and growth

YOUR NON-FICTION READING LIST

Period by Emma Barnett
guides readers through a journey of understanding,
providing insights and shedding light on the often-overlooked
aspects of women's experiences

The Argonauts by Maggie Nelson
offers an intellectually rich exploration of gender,
identity and family, intertwining personal narrative
with philosophical musings

Come as You Are by Emily Nagoski
offers an illuminating perspective on sexual well-being,
exploring the intricacies of desire and dispelling myths that
may hinder genuine understanding

All About Love by bell hooks
unravels the complexities of love, presenting a profound
exploration of its multifaceted nature and emphasising
its transformative potential

Love and Choice by Lucy Fry
presents a revolutionary viewpoint on relationships,
encouraging readers to reconsider societal norms and make
choices rooted in personal authenticity

HONEST: Everything They Don't Tell You About Sex...
by Milly Evans and Lucia Picerno
provides an unfiltered and candid portrayal of sex,
divulging information that is often omitted and fostering
a more open and informed perspective

The Sexual Revolution by Laurie Penny
traces the historical evolution of societal attitudes towards sex,
showcasing the transformative impact of this revolution on individual
and collective consciousness

The Big O by Oloni

sheds light on the intricacies of female pleasure, emphasising
the importance of understanding one's desires and fostering
a sense of empowerment

She Came to Stay by Simone de Beauvoir

navigates the complexities of relationships, delving into
themes of identity and existentialism in a narrative that
challenges conventional norms

Kink edited by R.O. Kwon and Garth Greenwell

provides a diverse exploration of sexual desire and practices,
showcasing a range of perspectives and experiences

Your Sexual Self by Lucy-Anne Holmes

guides readers on a journey of self-discovery, encouraging
a positive and empowering approach to understanding
one's sexual identity

Sex Talk by Olympe de G and Stephanie Estournet

delves into feminist perspectives on sexual empowerment,
fostering a dialogue around agency and autonomy

This is Pleasure by Mary Gaitskill

explores the nuances of power dynamics and consent
in intimate relationships, prompting readers to reflect on
societal norms and expectations

My Body by Emily Ratajkowski

offers a personal and empowering exploration of body
image and autonomy, encouraging readers to embrace
self-love and confidence

Pop Song by Larissa Pham

combines art and personal experiences to explore the
intersections of creativity and intimacy, offering a unique
lens on self-discovery

Body Work by Melissa Febos

advocates for the transformative potential of personal
narratives, emphasising the radical power of storytelling
in understanding and reclaiming one's body

Want Me by Tracy Clark-Flory

explores the complex and evolving landscape of female desire,
delving into societal expectations, personal experiences,
and the various facets that shape women's wants and needs

The Chain by Chimene Suleyman

is a memoir that exposes the control and betrayal of
one man over many women, celebrates the sisterhood
that emerged in response, and indicts the societal
misogyny that enables such manipulation.

7.

LGBTQIA+
IDENTITY

I could recommend queer books endlessly, forever. What began as an unconscious pattern of recommending queer authors to my friends transformed into a quiet awakening of my sense of self. It's precisely what stories do for us in all aspects of life. They whisper the words to us and we echo them back; we are seen, held, known. For many years, I found solace in my books. I felt ignited, life breathed into a furnace inside of me that had always been dimly lit; until I discovered Mina Loy, bell hooks, Torrey Peters, Julia Shaw, Virginia Woolf. It took many years, many chapters, many pages to feel this way, and it's what has fuelled a lifetime of recommending books to people that I believe have the power and passion to change their life, especially those by queer authors, for queer readers.

Queer books are a special kind of magic to me, they are a two-way conversation between writer and reader about the most intimate of subjects, one that you can have in secret, until you are ready to speak aloud. bell hooks said it best when she wrote:

'"Queer" not as being about who you're having sex with (that can be a dimension of it); but "queer" as being about the self that is at odds with everything around it and that has to invent and create and find a place to speak and to thrive and to live.'

So much of queer fiction and non-fiction is about carving out these spaces. Taking stories or archives of often demonised lifestyles, and showing us new ways to understand love and create a sense of belonging for our community.

ORLANDO
by Virginia Woolf

Many first literary greats began with creating fantastical spaces where characters explored sexuality, identity, sex and gender; and one that captivated me from the off was *Orlando* by Virginia Woolf. In an interview, writer Scarlett Curtis said, 'I feel the same way about Virginia Woolf that young girls feel about Harry Styles.'[xvii]

This felt like a fitting allegory to my ongoing love for Virginia Woolf as one of the first writers to open my eyes to queerness. Whilst moving through the strict heteronormative structures of Victorian society, Virginia Woolf wrote boldly about women with same-sex crushes, young men in Cambridge University society with homosexual desires, and fictionally about her own story with her lover Vita Sackville-West. The latter formed the first of Virginia Woolf's books I had ever read, *Orlando*, and it was where I fell richly in love with her.

Orlando was first published on 11 October 1928, impeccably beyond its time. A high-spirited romp inspired by the tumultuous family history of Woolf's lover and close friend, the aristocratic poet and novelist Vita Sackville-West, the book describes the adventures of a poet who changes sex and lives for centuries. Wholeheartedly considered a feminist classic, the book has been written about extensively by scholars of women's writing and LGBTQIA+ studies.

The book refuses to be contained within time, space and plot; it is about everything and nothing, and Orlando is the essence of fluidity, embracing all aspects of both (Woolf takes a binary view) in herself and her lovers: the differences are simultaneously profound and unremarked. When Orlando first realises he is now she, 'she showed no surprise'. *Orlando* embodies so much of what reading means to avid readers. It is a book that presents the ahead-of-its-time idea of being able to move through time and space and change one's gender identity at liberty and ease. A quote from the book reads: 'I'm sick to death of this particular self. I want another.' This always felt incredibly contemporary to me, and captures the euphoria of being able to step outside of the norm in an act of rebellion and in pursuit of being your true self. It's echoed in another of Woolf's novels, *Jacob's Room*, in the declaration, 'I am what I am, and intend to be it', which was utterly ahead of the cultural moment. The central message of *Orlando* is to be true to yourself, regardless of externally defined labels. Labels can be useful, but they should only ever be descriptive, not prescriptive.

DETRANSITION, BABY
by Torrey Peters

This is another queer book I am insufferable about in any bookish social circle. It is such an inspiring piece of queer literature that challenges traditional notions of gender, parenthood and family dynamics. Peters dedicates the book to divorced women and trans women, who are both on a profound journey of self-discovery akin to a rebirth. This dedication sets the tone for a narrative that intricately explores identity, relationships and the complexities of existence beyond societal binaries. The novel, a whip-smart debut, revolves around three women – transgender and cisgender – whose lives collide in unexpected ways when an unplanned pregnancy forces them to confront their deepest desires around gender, motherhood and sex. The protagonist, Reese, grapples with the complexities of her relationship with Amy, who detransitions and becomes Ames, setting off a series of life-altering events. Reese's character, caught in a self-destructive pattern, engages with the loneliness and explores unconventional avenues of connection.

What makes *Detransition, Baby* stand out is its ability to open minds to the idea of parenthood away from gender binaries and the conventional labels of 'mum' and 'dad'. Torrey Peters carefully crafts characters whose experiences resonate with authenticity, challenging societal expectations around family structures. The dedication to divorced women and trans women becomes a guiding principle in the narrative, emphasising the novel's commitment to portraying diverse journeys of self-discovery and resilience.

Torrey Peters doesn't write this novel to educate cisgender readers but rather to offer a rich and nuanced exploration of the emotional, messy and vulnerable corners of womanhood. The narrative unfolds fearlessly, navigating through dangerous taboos around gender, sex and relationships. The novel invites readers to question and reimagine the possibilities of queer family and parenthood, breaking free from heteronormative norms. As Roxane Gay aptly puts it in her review, *Detransition, Baby* is 'chaotic, well-written, gorgeously queer, messy, sex, and thought-provoking, addressing complex questions about womanhood, motherhood, fatherhood, and queer parenting.'

BI
by Julia Shaw

This is a book that takes the reader on a captivating journey through the intricate history of bisexuality, shedding light on the diverse ways in which queerness has been explored and tested throughout time. Put simply, as a bisexual woman, this was one of the singular times I felt *seen* in a non-fiction book. The exploration of the historical roots of modern sexuality terminology is not only enlightening but also mind-opening, offering a nuanced perspective on the evolution of sexual identities. Shaw, in her academic yet engaging style, presents a comprehensive introduction to the history of bisexuality, unveiling a treasure trove of facts and statistics that often remain overlooked.

Bi serves as a vital platform for the visibility of bisexuality, a sexual orientation frequently marginalised by both heterosexual and queer communities. Shaw courageously tackles the difficult chapters, vividly depicting the oppression faced by bisexual individuals. While these sections may be challenging to digest, they are a necessary exploration into the struggles and triumphs of bisexual folx, contributing to a more complete understanding of this often-neglected aspect of human sexuality.

Despite its academic nature, *Bi* doesn't solely dwell on the challenges but delves into the joys of identifying as bisexual, finding community and experiencing the validation of one's identity. The narrative emphasises that excluding bisexuality from discussions surrounding history, culture or science diminishes the vast spectrum of human love and attraction. Shaw beautifully encapsulates this sentiment in her poignant quote, 'To exclude bisexuality from discussions of history, culture or science is to belittle the human capacity for love and attraction. It also means that people with bisexual desires are often left abandoned in their search for a place in the world.' Through its meticulous exploration and celebration of bisexuality, *Bi* not only fills a crucial gap in LGBTQIA+ literature but also offers a powerful narrative for those curious about their own identities, beckoning readers to embrace the richness and diversity of human sexuality.

ROSEWATER
by Liv Little

Whenever I begin talking about this book (usually imposing it on friends and family as my new favourite queer read), I have to begin with an inhale of breath. As a queer person, there is just so much I could say about this novel and how it accurately depicts the lived experience of messy millennial bisexuality. *Rosewater* is a powerful coming-of-age narrative that transcends the conventional boundaries of friendship, community and the exploration of identity. Little masterfully crafts a vibrant tapestry of characters predominantly centred around queer Caribbean individuals navigating the bustling city of London. As someone intimately connected to the age group portrayed in the novel, I found myself reflecting on the notion of when precisely the coming-of-age period should be situated in literature. Little's choice to illuminate the transformation during the late twenties resonated deeply with me, mirroring the significant life decisions and evolving perspectives that characterise this tumultuous yet transformative time.

The novel unfolds as a beautiful, queer 'friends to lovers' tale, showcasing the messy and authentic aspects of millennial romance. Little ingeniously incorporates her experiences as the founder and editor of *gal-dem*, highlighting the importance of the arts and poetry in the characters' lives. Through Elsie's narrative, queerness takes centre stage, seamlessly intertwining with elements of class, race and feminism, breathing life into characters who unapologetically embody their multifaceted identities.

Rosewater emerges as a celebration of queer love and found family, both sensual and dynamic while grounded in authenticity. Little's narrative serves as a rallying cry for lovers and poets alike, igniting a fire within the pages that captivates and emboldens readers. The magnetic connection between the two main characters, their shared experiences of watching *RuPaul's Drag Race*, and the transformative power of their unity create a narrative richness that resonates. Even as the characters navigate divergent paths, the strength of their bond permeates the novel, leaving an indelible mark on the reader's heart. Little's exploration of friendship, queerness and the complexities of identity in *Rosewater* is a testament to the transformative and empowering potential of literature.

BELLIES
by Nicola Dinan

A compelling exploration of human connection, intimacy, hunger and changing identity, *Bellies* is profound and moving, and unfolds under the masterful pen of a debut trans author of colour. Drawing comparisons to the unwavering honesty of Sally Rooney's *Normal People* and the heart-wrenching depth of Hanya Yanagihara's *A Little Life*,

Dinan's novel stands on its own as a unique and resonant work. The author's trans identity brings a nuanced and authentic perspective to the narrative, offering readers an intimate and empathetic glimpse into the complexities of self-discovery and queer relationships in the modern age.

The title, *Bellies*, encapsulates the novel's essence, drawing on the act of revealing one's belly as an animalistic gesture of trust – a soft, vulnerable part of the body that is protected instinctively. Dinan weaves a tapestry of connections that mirror this vulnerability, illustrating the acts of friendship and intimacy that allow individuals to metaphorically show their bellies. The narrative unfolds with the characters, Tom and Ming, navigating their evolving identities – Tom reconciling his sexuality as a gay man in the unexpected realm of love with a woman, and Ming grappling with her own journey from living as a gay man to accepting herself as a straight woman. *Bellies* delicately explores their growing pains, offering a gentle yet incisive portrayal of the complexities inherent in personal discovery.

Dinan's storytelling is a testament to humanity, presenting an unflinchingly honest portrayal of the struggles and triumphs of becoming one's authentic self. The characters, whether central protagonists or members of their interconnected circles, are rendered with remarkable compassion and depth. Dinan's debut stands as a beacon of contemporary literature, providing a narrative that is not only moving and humane but also pushes the boundaries of understanding and empathy in the exploration of queer identities and relationships.

SISTER OUTSIDER
by Audre Lorde

This book stands as an essential piece of non-fiction, providing a profound exploration of Black feminism and Black queerness that has been instrumental in paving the way for the freedoms we enjoy today. In her words, 'The move to render the presence of lesbians and gay men invisible in the intricate fabric of Black existence and survival is a move which contributes to fragmentation and weakness in the black community.' This quote encapsulates the urgency of recognising and celebrating the diverse experiences within the Black community, particularly those of queer individuals whose visibility is essential to its strength.

Lorde's collection of essays is a powerful and insightful journey into her roles as a Black, lesbian, feminist poet and thinker. Her words serve as a timeless reminder of the interconnectedness of oppressions and the necessity of solidarity. Another poignant quote declares, 'I am a lesbian woman of Color whose children eat regularly because I work in a university. If their full bellies make me fail to recognize my commonality with a woman of Color whose children do not eat because she cannot find work, or who has no children because her insides are rotted from home abortions and sterilization; if I fail to recognize the lesbian who chooses not to have children, the woman who remains closeted because her homophobic community is her only life support, the woman who chooses silence instead of another death, the woman who is terrified lest my anger trigger the explosion of hers; if I fail to recognize them as other faces of myself, then I am contributing not only to each of their oppressions but also to my own, and the anger which stands between us then must be used for clarity and mutual empowerment, not for evasion by guilt or for further separation.'

Frequently, while reading, one can discern the threads of thought and arguments that have carried into more recent works of antiracist or intersectional feminist literature. Lorde's discussions about her queerness are intentionally designed to resonate with a wider audience than only queer women, expressing a deep care for the bonds of sisterhood and the transformative power of people coming together, even if that care has sometimes led to profound pain. *Sister Outsider* is not just a historical cornerstone but also an illuminating guide for those curious about their own identities, urging readers to confront their roles in perpetuating oppression and inspiring them to contribute to the ongoing struggle for justice and equality.

YOUR FICTION READING LIST

Lush Lives by J. Vanessa Lyon
presents a kaleidoscopic exploration of queer existence, unveiling
the intricacies of lives that defy societal norms and expectations

Easier Ways To Say I Love You by Lucy Fry
beautifully illustrates the diverse ways in which love manifests
within the LGBTQIA+ community

My Policeman by Bethan Roberts
delves into the complexities of love and desire against the
backdrop of societal expectations, portraying the challenges
faced by queer individuals in navigating their identities

Any Other City by Hazel Jane Plante
showcases a vibrant cityscape where characters
navigate the nuances of queerness

Biography of X by Catherine Lacey
unfolds a mesmerising narrative that illuminates the unique journey of
self-discovery and self-definition within the queer spectrum

Glassworks by Olivia Wolfgang-Smith
intricately weaves together tales that intersect with the
LGBTQIA+ community, offering a mosaic of experiences that
challenge and redefine traditional narratives

Homebodies by Tembe Denton-Hurst
delves into the personal spaces and intimate lives of queer individuals,
portraying the richness and diversity of home and chosen family

The Fifth Wound by Aurora Mattia
explores themes of queerness, spirituality and identity,
creating a tapestry that reflects the multifaceted nature of
the LGBTQIA+ community

A Manual for How to Love Us by Erin Slaughter
offers an intimate exploration of love within the queer community,
providing insights into the varied ways in which individuals
express and receive love

Natural Beauty by Ling Ling Huang
celebrates the diverse forms of beauty, emphasising
self-expression and individuality

Pomegranate by Helen Elaine Lee
explores the LGBTQIA+ experience through a lens of intersectionality,
addressing the complex layers of identity and community

Your Driver Is Waiting by Priya Guns
traverses the emotional landscapes of queer lives, revealing
resilience and strength

Scorched Grace by Margot Douaihy
delves into the intricacies of queer experiences, weaving together stories
that celebrate the beauty and resilience of LGBTQIA+ individuals

The Color Purple by Alice Walker
presents a timeless narrative that includes a profound
exploration of queer relationships

Oranges Are Not the Only Fruit by Jeanette Winterson
unravels a captivating tale that offers a poignant
reflection on selfhood

Cherry Beach by Laura McPhee-Browne
unfolds a narrative that intricately intertwines the lives
of queer characters, providing a glimpse into the joys
and challenges of LGBTQIA+ relationships

Paul Takes the Form of a Mortal Girl by Andrea Lawlor
explores the fluidity of gender and desire, showcasing the kaleidoscopic
nature of queer experiences

A Lonely Girl is a Dangerous Thing by Jessie Tu
delves into the intricacies of selfhood, offering a poignant
exploration of the challenges faced by queer individuals
in finding their place in the world

We Do What We Do in The Dark by Michelle Hart
unravels a suspenseful narrative that incorporates elements of queerness,
adding complexity to the characters and highlighting diversity

Sirens & Muses by Antonia Angress
offers an exploration of creativity and identity within the LGBTQIA+
community, showcasing the vibrant tapestry of queer experiences

They're Going to Love You by Meg Howrey
intricately weaves together stories of love and connection

Dykette by Jenny Fran Davis
explores the nuances of queer identity, capturing the unique experiences
of LGBTQIA+ individuals as they navigate self-discovery

After Sappho by Selby Wynn Schwartz
beautifully honours the legacy of Sappho, delving into the rich
history of queer voices and contributions to literature, celebrating the
enduring spirit of LGBTQIA+ creativity

The Queens of Sarmiento Park by Camila Sosa Villada
presents a compelling narrative that explores the lives of drag queens,
offering a glimpse into the vibrant and diverse world of queer performance

Lesbian Love Story by Amelia Possanza
provides an intimate portrayal of queer love, capturing the depth and
complexity of relationships within the LGBTQIA+ community

Freshwater by Akwaeke Emezi
explores the intersections of identity and queerness, delivering a
narrative that transcends conventional boundaries and delves into the
complexities of the human experience

Afterlove by Tanya Byrne
delves into themes of love and loss between two queer women

Felix Ever After by Kacen Callender
unfolds a heart-warming narrative that centres around the experiences
of a transgender protagonist, contributing to the growing body of literature
that amplifies transgender voices

Last Night at the Telegraph Club by Malinda Lo
offers a historical exploration of queer identities, providing a nuanced
portrayal of LGBTQIA+ experiences against the backdrop of
mid-twentieth-century America

On Earth We're Briefly Gorgeous by Ocean Vuong
presents a lyrical and poignant exploration of queerness, family and identity,
contributing to the rich tapestry of queer literature

In the Dream House by Carmen Maria Machado
offers a groundbreaking exploration of queer domestic violence,
challenging preconceived notions and contributing to a vital conversation
within the LGBTQIA+ community

Mrs Dalloway by Virginia Woolf

offers up a literary masterpiece, with subtle explorations
of queerness and non-normative identities, showcasing Woolf's
nuanced understanding of the human psyche

Kissing the Witch by Emma Donoghue

takes readers on a fantastical journey through
reimagined fairy tales, exploring themes of queerness,
transformation and identity

The Future by Naomi Alderman

explores speculative futures with queer elements,
contributing to conversations about the potential evolution
of societal norms surrounding gender and sexuality

The Lesbiana's Guide to Catholic School by Sonora Reyes

provides a witty and insightful exploration of queer experiences
within the framework of Catholic education, offering a unique
perspective on identity and faith

Neon Roses by Rachel Dawson

offers a poetic exploration of queerness, love and identity,
intertwining themes that resonate within the LGBTQIA+ community

Wild Things by Laura Kay

engages with the complexities of queer relationships, portraying the
beauty and challenges faced in navigating love and connection

Her Majesty's Royal Coven by Juno Dawson
presents a whimsical narrative that combines queerness with
magic and royalty, offering a delightful exploration of
queer characters within a fantastical realm

Rubyfruit Jungle by Rita Mae Brown
stands as a classic in queer literature, providing a spirited
and humorous narrative that explores themes of identity
and self-discovery

A Love Story for Bewildered Girls by Emma Morgan
weaves a tale exploring the complexities of love and identity
through the lives of three women navigating their way
through modern relationships

Mr. Loverman by Bernardine Evaristo
delves into the life of an older Caribbean man living in London,
grappling with his hidden homosexuality and the impact
of this on his family

All-night Pharmacy by Ruth Madievsky
explores the intricacies of human experiences, blending vulnerability
and strength in its exploration of love, loss and self-discovery

Endpapers by Jennifer Savran Kelly
presents a poignant exploration of family dynamics,
loss and the endurance of queer love through the lens
of a rare-book conservator

YOUR NON-FICTION READING LIST

Ace by Angela Chen

explores the diverse experiences of asexuality, delving into the meaning
of sex, desire and their implications for individuals and society

The Fixed Stars by Molly Wizenberg

reflects on the author's journey of self-discovery and identity, grappling
with the complexities of desire and changing perspectives

Zami: A New Spelling of My Name by Audre Lorde

beautifully captures Lorde's journey as a Black lesbian woman,
highlighting her exploration of identity, love and self-discovery

The Essential Dykes To Watch Out For by Alison Bechdel

chronicles the lives of a diverse group of lesbians, offering a humorous
and insightful commentary on the LGBTQIA+ community

Untamed by Glennon Doyle

explores Doyle's journey towards self-discovery, dismantling societal
expectations and embracing authenticity in love and life

100 Queer Poems edited by Andrew McMillan, Mary Jean Chan

celebrates the richness and complexity of queer
experiences through the power of poetry

Life as a Unicorn by Amrou Al-Kadhi
provides a captivating and humorous exploration of the
author's life as a queer Muslim and drag queen

None of the Above by Travis Alabanza
examines seven sentences that people have directed at them
about their gender identity and how society can go beyond the binary
way of thinking to expand our world view and acceptance

What's the T? by Juno Dawson
delves into the language, culture and history of the
LGBTQIA+ community

This Book is Gay by Juno Dawson
offers valuable insights into LGBTQIA+ identities,
relationships and community

A Trans Man Walks Into A Gay Bar by Harry Nicholas
shares personal experiences as a trans man navigating
the LGBTQIA+ scene, offering a unique perspective on
identity and acceptance

Queer Life, Queer Love edited by Matt Bates,
Golnoosh Nour, Sarah & Kate Bea
will be a once-in-a-lifetime read, an anthology that explores
the multifaceted aspects of queer life and love, featuring diverse
voices and stories

Beyond the Gender Binary by Alok Vaid-Menon
challenges and deconstructs the traditional gender binary,
offering a perspective that embraces fluidity and inclusivity

The Book of Queer Prophets curated by Ruth Hart
amplifies the voices of queer visionaries, showcasing diverse
perspectives on spirituality, identity and activism

Greedy by Jen Winston
explores the concept of greediness in reclaiming space,
pleasure and joy as queer individuals

Queer Sex by Juno Roche
provides a comprehensive and inclusive guide to queer sex,
addressing the unique experiences of trans and non-binary individuals

A Girlhood: A Letter to my Transgender Daughter
by Carolyn Hays
shares a love letter from a mother to a child who has always known
herself and is waiting for the rest of the world to catch up

Pageboy by Elliot Page
delves into Page's personal journey of self-discovery, fame
and embracing his transgender identity

Trans Sex: A Guide for Adults by Kelvin Sparks
offers a practical guide addressing the sexual health
and experiences of transgender individuals, fostering a more
inclusive and informed dialogue

Beyond Monogamy by Mimi Schippers
explores the challenges and possibilities of non-monogamous
relationships, challenging traditional notions of love and commitment

Homosexuality: Power and Politics by the Gay Left Collective
delves into the complex intersections of homosexuality,
power dynamics and political activism

Queer by Frank Wynne
provides a comprehensive examination of queer history,
culture and identity, offering a rich and informative narrative

Gender Magic by Rae McDaniel
explores the transformative power of gender expression and identity,
providing insights and guidance for those on their gender journey

Ace by Angela Chen
investigates the diverse landscape of asexuality, unravelling its
implications for desire, societal norms and the very concept of sex

Polysecure by Jessica Fern
explores the intersection of attachment theory, trauma and
consensual non-monogamy, providing insights into creating secure
relationships in diverse romantic structures

The Radicality of Love by Srećko Horvat
explores the radical potential of love as a force for
societal change, questioning conventional norms
and advocating for a more compassionate world

Working-class Queers by Yvette Taylor
examines the intersection of class and queerness, shedding
light on the experiences of working-class LGBTQIA+ individuals

Supporting Trans People of Colour by Sabah Choudrey
provides practical insights and guidance on supporting trans
people of colour, addressing the unique challenges they face

We Have Always Been Here by Samra Habib
chronicles Habib's journey as a queer Muslim woman,
exploring the intersections of faith, identity and love

Girls Can Kiss Now by Jill Gutowitz
offers a humorous and insightful take on the
experiences of queer women, navigating love,
relationships and societal expectations

8.

New Beginnings

There are times in a reader's life when the book you read is the book you *need*. It spoke to you from the bookshop shelf, called at you from the library, and for one reason or another, you were compelled to pick it up. What you begin to realise, a few pages in, is that this book found you at exactly the right time in your life. It ties so perfectly with the hand you've been dealt, your struggles of the moment, and it offers solace, guidance and friendship. This can be felt acutely when we find ourselves at a crossroads, on the cusp of a big change or a new direction, or a more general implosion of The Plan.

We have all experienced moments when everything appears to be going according to The Plan, and then suddenly, without warning, something goes spectacularly 'wrong'. I use the word wrong in inverted commas, because I am a firm believer that what is meant for you won't miss you, and the many times in life when we feel derailed, we are actually being course corrected, gently directed towards a path more fitting for us. So whether you've found yourself in a very one-sided breakup, left reeling from redundancy at your dream job, or any matter of circumstances covered by Alanis Morissette's 'Ironic', know there are most certainly books to help you feel less alone, and there are even books that will light the way to your next evolution of personhood.

I'm going to bypass any metaphors of chrysalises, phoenix and the like, but I take comfort in the fact that any time I've found myself in a pit of despair wondering why my life, when all seemed to be perfectly in balance, was suddenly knocked off course, I have found myself in a better place afterwards. These trials and tribulations can come at any time – they're not limited to early adulthood, even though they often make us return to an adolescent state, suddenly we are children on the phone to our parents insisting we have no idea what to do. The truth, I've found at least, is that sometimes life has to fall apart spectacularly in order for you to find yourself taking a path you would not have sought out unless pushed to your extremities. Fight or flight kicks in, and taking a bet on yourself, or on a dream that felt too out of reach before, suddenly feels less frightening. It's often easier to jump into an unknown that looks a lot like oblivion when you feel you've lost almost everything already.

Being introduced to the right book can therefore completely alter the course of our lives. Whether non-fiction or fiction, they hold the key to show us a version of life we perhaps had never imagined for ourselves, or thought possible. The books I've listed here are ones I have recommended time and time again to people who find themselves at a crossroads, unsure of where to turn, and asking for a book to guide or support them. Change is scary, anthropologically we panic over it and our brains try to tell us we're being chased by a predator, but it's grounding to read the words of someone who has gone through momentous challenge and change to come out the other side a truer and more authentic version of themselves. Novels show us that we too are continual works in progress.

HIS ONLY WIFE
by Peace Adzo Medie

The narrative of this book unfolds as a tale of gradual empowerment and learning, challenging the constructs of traditionalism and marriage. *His Only Wife* delves into the lives of disobedient women, and Medie skilfully navigates the complexities of characters who resist conformity. The story introduces Afi Tekple, a young seamstress in a small Ghanaian town, poised to marry a man she has never met. The groom, Eli, fails to show up at their wedding due to a business trip, setting the stage for a transformative journey for Afi.

Moving to Accra, Afi steps into a life that contrasts starkly with her humble origins – a fancy new apartment, a personal driver and the commencement of her apprenticeship as a fashion designer. All the while, she navigates the intricacies of her marriage to Eli, who already has another woman and a child in close proximity. Despite the unconventional circumstances, Afi's character stands out for her pure heart and unwavering sense of self. In a role that could easily diminish a woman's agency, given she is essentially a bought bride tasked with breaking up an existing relationship, Afi's resilience shines through. In a city as vast as Accra, filled with dreams and aspirations, Afi embarks on a journey of self-discovery, defying expectations and discovering the true meaning of freedom.

His Only Wife transcends the typical narrative of arranged marriages and societal expectations. Afi becomes a symbol of a woman who refuses to be confined by predetermined roles, challenging the expectations imposed upon her. Medie's debut novel is not only a captivating tale of a woman navigating big life changes but also a powerful exploration of autonomy and the pursuit of one's identity in the face of societal constraints. It is a narrative that lingers in the reader's thoughts long after the pages have been turned, prompting reflection on the transformative power of individual agency and the courage to define one's path.

YOU MADE A FOOL OF DEATH
WITH YOUR BEAUTY
by Akwaeke Emezi

With beauty in the name, this book essentially makes that its promise: exploring how beauty can be found again after even the greatest of challenges. Akwaeke Emezi's second book emerges as a captivating exploration of big life changes, preparing for the next chapter and navigating life-altering shifts. The narrative centres around Feyi, who, five years after a tragic accident claimed the love of her life, undergoes a remarkable transformation. Now an artist with her own studio, sharing a brownstone apartment with her steadfast friend Joy, Feyi is encouraged by Joy to re-enter the dating scene. Unprepared for anything serious, Feyi finds herself entangled in a whirlwind summer romance after a steamy encounter at a rooftop party. What follows is a journey of self-discovery, luxury trips to tropical islands, decadent meals and professional opportunities that open unforeseen doors.

The narrative delves into Feyi's internal conflict as she navigates a burgeoning relationship while feeling the dangerous allure of someone off-limits. The book grapples with complex questions: How does one honour grief while embracing the future? Who is Feyi ready to become, and how far is she willing to go for a second chance at love? The quote, 'He loved people being messy as fuck – he said it was one of the best things about being human, how we could make such disasters and recover from them enough to make them into stories later,' underscores the book's celebration of the messy, intricate nature of human existence and our ability to weave stories from chaos.

Feyi emerges as a resilient and strong lead, navigating life with agency after the profound loss that marked her past. The narrative unfolds sensually, capturing not only the intimate aspects of Feyi's life but also the sensory richness of her experiences – be it in the realms of food, music or the vibrant foliage that surrounds her. Feyi's journey becomes

a multisensory reawakening, a testament to her growing confidence as she emerges from trauma, engaging with life again in a way that is both inspiring and beautiful. Emezi's novel becomes a celebration of resilience, transformation and the complexity of human emotion in the face of profound change.

MAAME
by Jessica George

This novel invites readers into the transformative journey of Maddie, a young woman navigating the intricate tapestry of life's challenges, big changes and profound shifts. The narrative unfolds in London, where Maddie finds herself grappling with the responsibilities of being the primary caretaker for her father, who is battling advanced-stage Parkinson's, and contending with a demanding boss at work. Eager for a change, Maddie seizes the opportunity when her mother returns from Ghana. A self-proclaimed late-bloomer, she embarks on a quest for meaningful 'firsts': a new flat, after-work drinks, career recognition and the complexities of internet dating.

As the story progresses, readers follow Maddie through the ebbs and flows of professional challenges, forging new friendships and navigating the intricacies of romantic relationships. Naïve and inexperienced, Maddie grapples with finding equilibrium amid life's demands. Tragedy strikes, casting Maddie into a vortex of guilt and loss. It is in these moments of despair that Maddie begins to comprehend the significance of prioritising herself, confronting those who have taken her for granted, and embracing the complexities of her unconventional family.

Maame is not just a novel; it is a moving and deeply insightful exploration of family dynamics, grief, self-growth, guilt and the pursuit of happiness. The narrative is enriched by George's excellent writing and superb characterisations. Maddie's nickname, *Maame*, meaning 'woman' in Twi, becomes a focal point as she reflects on its influence in shaping her perceptions of herself and her interactions with others. The novel weaves a poignant melody, addressing themes of family, grief, sexuality and the search for happiness in a truly inspirational and memorable manner.

George's debut is a remarkable bildungsroman, capturing the essence of life's ever-evolving journey with authenticity and emotion. *Maame* is an incredible work that delves into the complexities of grief, dysfunctional family relationships, workplace challenges and self-discovery. The character of Maddie shines as she faces life's challenges, becoming a beacon of acknowledgment, acceptance and confidence in her glorious differences. With its genuine and realistic approach, *Maame* is a beautiful and effortless debut that resonates deeply with readers.

Envision yourself standing at the cusp of your twenties, a heady cocktail of anticipation and trepidation swirling within. It is like being given the keys to a brand-new car, having never driven before in your life. Enter Elizabeth Day's book *How to Fail*, a welcome guide poised to unveil the truth behind how failure can be our best navigation system yet. Elizabeth Day assumes the mantle of a sage confidante, orchestrating intimate conversation over steaming cups of coffee, recounting her own fumbles and stumbles. If you've listened to her podcast of the same name, you'll know this to be true. She unfurls the artistry within failure, ensuring us that every failure is simply a redirection to our true and authentic path in life. *How to Fail* becomes your raison d'etre – a literary embrace reassuring us that uncertainty is part of life. Here's to traversing the scenic route and enfolding the tumult with arms flung wide, because, ultimately, it is the deviations from our intended paths that make for the best journeys.

YOUR FICTION READING LIST

Really Good Actually by Monica Heisey
will make you laugh and cry as you inhale the story
of a young divorcee getting back to herself

Either/Or by Elif Batuman
weaves a captivating narrative exploring the complexities
of love, language and identity in this poignant novel

White Teeth by Zadie Smith
delves into the intertwined lives of two families, spanning generations
and continents, while tackling themes of identity, multiculturalism
and the human condition

Tomorrow, and Tomorrow, and Tomorrow by Gabrielle Zevin
crafts a thought-provoking tale that examines the intricacies of love,
loss and the profound impact of technology on our lives

Conversations with Friends by Sally Rooney
explores the nuances of friendship, love and ambition in
a modern setting, delivering a raw and introspective narrative

Crying in H Mart by Michelle Zauner
offers a poignant exploration of grief, identity and the
deep connection between food and culture

Fates and Furies by Lauren Groff
unravels the intricacies of a marriage, presenting a dual perspective
that peels back the layers of love, deception and personal truths

The Lonely Londoners by Sam Selvon
paints a vivid picture of post-war London through the eyes of Caribbean
immigrants, capturing the challenges and camaraderie of their experiences

Supper Club by Lara Williams
explores the liberating and rebellious act of women reclaiming their
bodies and appetites through the unconventional Supper Club

Animals by Emma Jane Unsworth
offers a humorous and honest portrayal of female friendship,
hedonism and the struggles of adulthood

In Five Years by Rebecca Serle
navigates the complexities of destiny, love and self-discovery
when a woman experiences a glimpse into her future in a dream

The Secret History by Donna Tartt
provides a mesmerising tale of murder, academia and the
unravelling of a close-knit group of eccentric students

The Namesake by Jhumpa Lahiri
weaves a poignant exploration of identity, culture and the immigrant
experience through the lens of a young man named Gogol Ganguli

The Rachel Papers by Martin Amis
offers a darkly comedic and introspective look at the life of an
ambitious and self-absorbed young man

Quicksand by Nella Larsen
explores the struggles of Helga Crane, a biracial woman
navigating societal expectations and personal identity
in the early twentieth century

I Love Dick by Chris Kraus
delves into the complexities of desire, obsession and the
blurred lines between fiction and reality

YOUR NON-FICTION READING LIST

The Skills by Mishal Husain
imparts valuable insights and wisdom, offering practical
guidance for personal and professional growth

Money by Laura Whateley
will change your relationship with finance, and help you to bolster
control over money in challenging and uncertain times

The Success Myth by Emma Gannon
challenges you to rethink your goals and what you gain from
constant stress and work, when you could lean into a slower,
more intentional way of living instead

Work Won't Love You Back by Sarah Jaffe
helps you detach from capitalism and promotion as the ultimate
goal, and refocus on family, fulfilment and joy

Playing Big by Tara Mohr
empowers women to overcome self-doubt and embrace their full
potential, offering strategies for personal and professional success

How to Own the Room by Viv Groskop
provides a guide to confidence and impactful communication,
empowering individuals to harness their presence and influence

Set Boundaries, Find Peace by Nedra Glover Tawwab
explores the importance of setting boundaries for personal
well-being and achieving inner peace

Crying in the Bathroom by Erika L. Sánchez
delves into the emotional challenges of adulthood, offering a candid and
relatable exploration of personal struggles

Buy Yourself the F*cking Lilies by Tara Schuster
advocates for self-love and care, providing a humorous and
empowering guide to personal well-being

Stay True by Hua Hsu
explores the complexities of identity, culture and staying true to oneself

How to Do Nothing by Jenny Odell
challenges the culture of productivity and explores the
art of intentional living

The Source of Self-regard by Toni Morrison
delves into themes of race, identity and literature with profound insight

Into the Wild by Jon Krakauer
recounts the gripping and tragic true story of Chris McCandless,
who ventured into the Alaskan wilderness seeking a profound
connection with nature

All the Gold Stars by Rainesford Stauffer
redefines ambition and explores societal expectations,
encouraging a reimagining of personal success

Revolution From Within by Gloria Steinem
imparts wisdom on self-empowerment and personal revolution,
offering a guide to inner transformation

The Book of Moods by Lauren Martin
shares her journey of turning negative emotions into a
positive life, inviting insights into emotional well-being

How to Be a Person in the World by Heather Havrilesky
offers thoughtful and humorous guidance on
navigating life's challenges

The Defining Decade by Meg Jay
explores the crucial decisions and experiences that shape one's
twenties, offering advice on making the most of this formative
period and grow to build the life you aspire to live

9.

new parents

In the whirlwind of pregnancy and the tumultuous journey of parenthood, finding solace in the pages of books becomes an invaluable refuge for both new and seasoned parents alike. While the demands of caring for a newborn or navigating the uncharted territories of parenting may leave little room for leisurely reading, the act of delving into literature on the subject becomes an essential lifeline. Embracing the wisdom and insights that parenting books offer can be a transformative experience, providing a compass for the journey of becoming and evolving as a parent.

In the chaotic symphony of parenting, books serve as mentors, offering guidance, empathy and a reservoir of knowledge to those navigating the labyrinth of parenthood. The books in this genre act as a gentle reminder that parenthood is a shared human experience, and the challenges faced are universal. From the sleepless nights of infancy to the delicate dance of discipline and love, these literary companions illuminate the multifaceted nature of parenting.

Moreover, engaging with literature on parenting and the relationships between parents and children extends beyond mere survival advice. It invites parents to embark on a journey of self-discovery and self-improvement, allowing them to break free from the mould of their own upbringing. The realm of bibliotherapy empowers parents to challenge traditional notions and embrace progressive approaches to parenting. By reading about different parenting styles, strategies and experiences, individuals can shape their own unique narrative, fostering an environment where both parent and child thrive.

As the pages turn, parents are offered the opportunity to explore the nuances of their own upbringing, questioning inherited norms and seeking avenues for growth. The gift of literature is not just in the words on the page; it lies in the expansion of one's perspective and the potential for positive transformation. While parenting may be an uncharted territory, the books on this subject act as trusted guides, providing the tools needed to sculpt a parenting style that resonates with individual values and aspirations. Through the art of reading, parents can redefine their narrative, paving the way for a more enriched, empathetic and harmonious relationship with their children.

ROOM TEMPERATURE
by Nicholson Baker

In the sacred stillness of a rocking chair, Nicholson Baker invites readers into the world of parenthood with his exquisite work, *Room Temperature*. In this novella-length fictionalised essay, Baker crafts a literary oasis that transcends the mundane and delves into the extraordinary beauty of a 20-minute episode – rocking his infant daughter to sleep. The narrative unfolds as a quiet, seriously charming piece of art, echoing the tactics Baker skilfully employed in *The*

Mezzanine. This time, the focus is on the domestic realm, an intimate exploration of a father's tender moments as he feeds and rocks his child.

Baker's prose, almost photorealistic in its precision, serves as a canvas for his gloriously obsessive attention to detail. While conventional plotlines take a back seat, the narrative bursts forth with poetic onslaughts, delivering a pyrotechnic display of technical prowess. Within this literary tapestry, the plot becomes secondary to the warmth and hilarity derived from the author's deeply human and loving portrayal of a father revelling in a quiet moment with his child. The narrative unfolds with a cadence that mirrors the rhythmic rocking, as Baker immerses readers in the profound yet simple joys of parenthood.

As readers embark on this literary journey, they find themselves not merely witnessing a father–daughter interaction but partaking in a celebration of the ordinary rendered extraordinary. Baker's exploration of the domestic landscape is an ode to the beauty inherent in the minutiae of life. *Room Temperature* stands as an ideal companion for new parents, offering a literary refuge that mirrors the tenderness, joy and humour of the early moments of parenting. Through Baker's lens, the act of rocking a child to sleep transforms into a symphony of emotions, inviting readers to cherish the subtleties of their own parenting odysseys.

MOTHER MOTHER
by Annie Macmanus

In the tapestry of life, where threads of love, loss and the relentless passage of time are woven together, Annie Macmanus crafts a powerful coming-of-age novel and an intimate family study titled *Mother Mother*. As readers embark on this literary journey, a provocative thought lingers in the air, questioning the cost of unconditional love and the pursuit of light within the shadows of life's darkest corners.

At the heart of the narrative is Mary, a young girl thrust into the complexities of womanhood as she becomes pregnant upon losing her virginity. *Mother Mother* gracefully dances between past and present, chronicling Mary's odyssey from a motherless girl to a woman navigating the turbulent waters of civil war-era Northern Ireland. The haunting landscape unfolds over almost four decades, revealing the intricate web of relationships that shape Mary's life – a life where the absence of a mother catapults her into a world where familial bonds strain under the weight of societal expectations.

Macmanus expertly captures the oppressive undercurrents of Northern Ireland, where women are told they are not enough and societal progress seems elusive. Against the backdrop of classism and sexism, Mary's journey reflects the resilience of women who must confront these deeply ingrained attitudes. The novel emerges as a testament to the indomitable spirit of those who persevere in the face of societal constraints, offering readers a glimpse into a world that may seem familiar yet remains uniquely shaped by its community.

Mother Mother transcends the narrative of a hardworking Irish woman, delving into themes of mental health, mystery, teenage pregnancy and the transformative nature of motherhood. Macmanus paints a poignant portrait, infusing the narrative with nostalgic realism and a beating heart. The novel becomes a mirror reflecting the unforgiving, lonely and underappreciated aspects of motherhood – a reminder of the strength inherent in women who navigate these challenging realms, enduring and prevailing against the odds.

STAY WITH ME
by Ayòbámi Adébáyò

Against the emotional backdrop of marriage and fertility, Ayòbámi Adébáyò paints a poignant portrait of a Nigerian couple's heart-wrenching and relentless journey to parenthood in her celebrated debut novel, *Stay With Me*. Set in Nigeria between the mid-1980s and 2008, the novel delves into the tortuous relationship between Yejide and Akin, unravelling a narrative that explores the profound sacrifices individuals make for the sake of family.

What struck me most profoundly about Adébáyò's narrative prowess is her ability to craft characters who are deeply flawed, aggravating and yet undeniably human. The novel captures Yejide's intense yearning for children, a desire that propels her into a desperate quest for motherhood. The emotional complexity of her journey, coupled with the societal pressures and judgments she faces, makes for a heartbreaking and infuriating exploration of the sacrifices demanded of women. Adébáyọ̀'s portrayal of Yejide's struggles transcends cultural boundaries, resonating universally with the challenges and expectations placed on women.

Yejide and Akin, a couple with contemporary views on marriage, find themselves ensnared in the traditions of polygamy that define their families. As their dreams of a shared life unravel in the face of infertility, desperation takes hold, leading to lies, secrets and familial interventions that strain the fabric of their union. Through the lens of Yejide and Akin's story, Adébáyọ̀ confronts the universal themes of longing, societal expectations and the sacrifices individuals are willing to endure for the elusive embrace of family.

Stay With Me is an electrifying novel of enormous emotional power that poses profound questions about the lengths we go to preserve the sanctity of family. Ayọ̀bámi Adébáyọ̀'s exploration of the human spirit, resilience and the complexities of relationships creates a literary masterpiece that resonates with readers, inviting them to reflect on the sacrifices demanded by love and the transformative power of parenthood.

A LIFE'S WORK: ON BECOMING A MOTHER
by Rachel Cusk

Rachel Cusk's memoir, *A Life's Work*, stands as a provocative exploration of the transformative journey into motherhood, capturing the essence of this life-altering experience with unapologetic candour. Delving into the nuances of early motherhood, the book navigates the maelstrom of emotions, societal expectations and personal identity shifts that accompany the arrival of a child. In this eloquent narrative, Cusk recounts her own venture into motherhood, a journey that defies idealised notions and lays bare the complex realities that often elude public discourse.

The book, while originally divisive, emerges as a poignant testament to the author's willingness to unravel the less-glamorous facets of parenting. As Cusk grapples with the challenges of pregnancy, childbirth, sleepless nights and societal expectations, she crafts a narrative that is both brutally honest and emotionally resonant. The unfiltered portrayal of her experiences, devoid of sentimentality, challenges the prevailing cultural narratives surrounding motherhood. Cusk confronts the dichotomy of emotions – exposing the unpleasant yet acknowledging the occasional moments of joy, creating a narrative that transcends the conventional boundaries of parenting literature.

What distinguishes *A Life's Work* is Cusk's ability to critique not just the personal struggles of motherhood but also the societal constructs that often shape the maternal experience. Through her introspective lens, she dissects the cultural expectations and the pressures placed upon mothers, revealing the internal conflict faced in reconciling personal identity with the demands of parenting. The quote, 'To be a mother I must leave the telephone unanswered, work undone, arrangements unmet. To be myself I must let the baby cry, must forestall her hunger or leave her for evenings out, must forget her in order to think about other things,' encapsulates the heart of this struggle – a poignant reflection on the perpetual negotiation between the self and the role of a mother.

In navigating the turbulent waters of motherhood, Cusk's memoir serves as a timeless exploration for new parents and those contemplating the intricate dance between personal identity and the transformative journey of raising a child. The enduring relevance of *A Life's Work* lies in its capacity to spark conversations around the uncharted territories of parenthood, prompting readers to reflect on the profound, messy and beautifully imperfect nature of the maternal experience.

YOUR FICTION READING LIST

The School for Good Mothers by Jessamine Chan
explores societal expectations and the challenges of motherhood,
offering a nuanced narrative on parenting

The Mothers by Brit Bennett
weaves together the stories of multiple women, exploring themes of
identity, family and the complexities of motherhood

Detransition, Baby by Torrey Peters
delves into themes of gender, identity and relationships, offering a thought-
provoking narrative on what it means to parent beyond the gender binary

You Be Mother by Meg Mason
explores the intricacies of motherhood and family dynamics,
providing a heartfelt and relatable story of young motherhood

Such a Fun Age by Kiley Reid
addresses issues of race and privilege, providing a satirical and insightful take
on contemporary society against the backdrop of being a nanny

To Kill A Mockingbird by Harper Lee
explores racial injustice and moral growth in the American South through the eyes
of a young girl, and features one of the most iconic literary fathers, Atticus Finch

The Nursery by Szilvia Molnar
paints an honest, frightening and claustrophobic picture of new motherhood

After Birth by Elisa Albert
offers a candid and honest exploration of postpartum experiences,
addressing the challenges and joys of early motherhood

Olive by Emma Gannon
presents a modern exploration of identity and relationships,
offering a character-driven narrative exploring the choice
to become a parent or not

Little Labours by Rivka Galchen
offers a collection of essays that blend motherhood with literary
reflection, providing a unique perspective on parenting

That Kind of Mother by Rumaan Alam
addresses issues of race and privilege, providing a nuanced
exploration of motherhood and adoption

Look How Happy I'm Making You by Polly Rosenwaike
offers a collection of short stories that explore the complexities of motherhood

Well-behaved Indian Women by Saumya Dave
navigates the intergenerational complexities of mother-daughter
relationships, identity and the pursuit of individual dreams

Territory of Light by Yūko Tsushima
follows a woman's journey through single motherhood, exploring themes
of independence, isolation and the pursuit of personal identity

YOUR NON-FICTION READING LIST

Things That Helped by Jessica Friedmann
offers a collection of essays that blend personal experience
with broader cultural commentary providing insight into
mental health and motherhood

Nobody Told Me by Hollie McNish
explores the intersection of poetry and parenthood
offering a raw and honest reflection on the challenges
and joys of raising children

The Hungover Games by Sophie Heawood
combines humour and introspection, providing
a memoir that reflects on life's unexpected twists when
parenting was not on the cards

Matrescence by Lucy Jones
explores the psychological and emotional changes
of becoming a mother, offering insights into the
transformative journey of motherhood

The Queer Parent by Lotte Jeffs and Stu Oakley
provides a guide to queer parenting, offering advice and personal
narratives that reflect the diversity of queer family experiences

The Argonauts by Maggie Nelson
explores themes of love, identity and gender, offering a
genre-defying memoir that challenges traditional narratives

The Book of Mothers by Carrie Mullins
delves into the representation of motherhood
in literature, exploring how literary works can shape and redefine
contemporary notions of motherhood

Raising Them by Kyl Myers
offers a thoughtful exploration of raising children
outside traditional gender norms

***The Book You Wish Your Parents
Had Read*** by Philippa Perry
provides insights into effective parenting, offering guidance
on understanding and supporting children

The Little Book of Self-care for New Mums
by Alexis Stickland and Beccy Hands
shares insider tips from a midwife and doula on keeping yourself
comfortable, happy and calm in new motherhood

The Motherhood Affidavits by Laura Jean Baker
shares Baker's personal journey of motherhood,
providing a memoir that explores the complexities of parenting

The Art of Waiting by Belle Boggs
examines the intersection of fertility, medicine
and motherhood, offering a nuanced exploration of the
challenges faced by those trying to conceive

Mothermorphosis by Monica Dux
explores the transformative journey of becoming
a mother, offering reflections on the physical, emotional
and societal aspects of motherhood

Parenting Beyond Pink & Blue by Christia Spears Brown
provides a guide to raising children without
reinforcing gender stereotypes

A Slow Childhood by Helen Hayward
advocates for a thoughtful and intentional approach
to parenting, offering insights into how to create a nurturing
environment for children

Motherhood by Sheila Heti
presents a philosophical exploration of the decision to become a mother,
delving into questions of identity and purpose

Expecting Better by Emily Oster
challenges conventional pregnancy advice, offering
evidence-based insights into pregnancy choices

Mother Brain by Chelsea Conaboy
explores the intersection of neuroscience and parenthood,
offering a scientific perspective on the complexities of parenting

Like a Mother by Angela Garbes
combines feminist perspectives with scientific insights, providing
a holistic exploration of pregnancy

I Cannot Control Everything Forever by Emily C. Bloom
shares Bloom's personal journey of balancing
motherhood, science and art, providing a memoir that
intertwines these aspects of her life

Body Full of Stars by Molly Caro May
explores the emotional and physical transformations
of motherhood, reflecting on the intersection of female rage
and the passage into motherhood

Touched Out by Amanda Montei
addresses issues of motherhood, misogyny,
consent and control

Women Without Kids by Ruby Warrington
explores the experiences of women without children,
shedding light on the diverse paths and choices of those
who embrace a different narrative

And Now We Have Everything by Meaghan O'Connell
shares O'Connell's personal narrative of motherhood,
reflecting on the challenges of parenting when
one feels unprepared

Good Talk by Mira Jacob
navigates the challenges of interracial relationships,
parenthood and identity in a visually engaging
and emotionally resonant format

The Joys of Motherhood by Buchi Emecheta
explores the societal expectations and challenges faced by women
in Nigeria, focusing on the complexities of motherhood

10.

CREATIVITY
& INSPIRATION

I t's incredibly common for us to believe that creativity does not have a place in our adult lives. We've been told to value productivity and uniformity in our academic work, and admin that dominates our online jobs and lives. Creativity is so important for our mental well-being, and making the time to create art, literature, poetry, photography and anything in between is part of essential human connection.

A quote I return to when I feel like giving up on creative pursuits is this one from Sylvia Plath:

'And by the way, everything in life is writable about if you have the outgoing guts to do it, and the imagination to improvise. The worst enemy to creativity is self-doubt.'[xviii]

It is true, pursuing any creative path invites doubt, because it demands vulnerability. For someone guarded and people-pleasing, like me, this was scary enough a fact to keep me from writing for many years. I left off the creativity at university and renounced myself to having to engage with the 'real world', and that there was no practicality to my creativity. Still, I stole moments where I could, on scraps of till roll in my retail job to filling out pages with poetry and novel ideas in the back of my desk-job notebooks, but I confined these bursts of inspiration to these pages and nothing more. Putting these out into the world would mean I would have to be more honest, more intentional and more authentic. This was something I was simply not ready for, because doing so would alter the course of my life beyond recognition. It took me years of therapy, soul searching and purging of the toxicities from my life to get to a place where I felt compelled to exhale my creativity, and commit to it. Art takes courage, as all the great artists have told us of their works, and it is incredibly true. I'm consistently inspired by the number of my dear friends who have decided to take a chance on their creativity, ridding stability and corporate jobs for slight unstable but incredibly fulfilling creative opportunities, and with it, multiple streams of income and satisfaction you cannot get by doing anything else.

Creativity as a pursuit does not have to be a full-time job, it can be pursued in stolen moments or secret hours. It needn't be shouted about either; it can remain confined to our notes pages or scraps of paper stuffed into our coat pockets. You deserve more time to connect with your creativity than when you're on the bus. When you read that quote from Sylvia Plath, what stands out to you? What stares you in the face? What do you doubt about yourself? What is holding you back from committing more fully to your creativity? Ask yourself the question, yes, but find comfort in the words of Brenda Ueland in *If You Want to Write: Thoughts about Art, Independence and Spirit*, where she titles a chapter: 'Everybody is Talented, Original and Has Something Important to Say.'

If you're still doubtful, this is where bibliotherapy comes in. Like a rabbit from a hat, the right book, the right character, the right line of prose can surprise you and have you scrambling for a pen and paper, any medium to pour your soul onto. Engaging in art is such a vital part of creativity, but accessing inspiration in today's world is increasingly more difficult. How can we be expected to write a novel consisting of hundreds of pages, thousands of words, when our attention span is typically limited to thirty seconds, or three hundred characters on social media? How can we write from the very core of ourselves, when we're abashed by comparison culture, and lives that look 'better' than ours, more enviable, more exciting, more worthy of creating art about at the touch of a button? We too are so used to instant gratification and immediate results, but creativity doesn't happen fast, it is slow and needs to be nurtured. The very environment we engage with now pushes us further and further from creative capacity, but books and art bring us back. Natalie Goldberg, in *Writing Down the Bones: Freeing the Writer Within*, says: 'If you read good books, when you write, good books will come out of you. Maybe it's not quite that easy, but if you want to learn something, go to the source …'

Writers, artists and creatives alike all insist that the practice of innovation, inspiration and motivation that comes from engaging not only with the world (the Real World, offline) and art will bring forth our own creativity. Before I recommend a plethora of books that I have dog-eared and annotated throughout the years of my own creative pursuit, and been recommended by other creatives, I will leave you with this quote from Stephen King, to make my case that reading books (any books, but in this case, books *about* art and creativity), will get your creative juices flowing again:

'The real importance of reading is that it creates an ease and intimacy with the process of writing; one comes to the country of the writer with one's papers and identification pretty much in order. Constant reading will pull you into a place where you can write eagerly and without self-consciousness. "[R]ead a lot, write a lot" is the great commandment.' [xviii]

THE CHERRY ROBBERS
by Sarai Walker

This novel beckons readers into a world where creativity intertwines with a dark, gothic narrative. Inspired by the legacy of Georgia O'Keeffe, *The Cherry Robbers* tells the story of the enigmatic Sylvia Wren, an artist of immense importance in American art history. Fleeing her past for six decades, Sylvia faces a reckoning as a journalist threatens to expose her well-guarded secrets. The story unfurls through Sylvia's artist notebooks, revealing the haunting family curse that claimed the lives of her sisters, led her mother to an asylum, and forced Sylvia to abandon her former life.

This novel is a haunting, feminist tale that delves into themes of loneliness, grief and the impact of the past on the present. It emerges as a gloriously gothic thriller, capturing the essence of Margaret Atwood's storytelling prowess. The narrative not only explores the darkness within Sylvia's history but also serves as a vehicle for readers to engage with their own creative instincts. Through vivid depictions and dreamlike historical fiction, *The Cherry Robbers* is a fairy tale that unfolds against the backdrop of mid-century New York, weaving Gothic-tinged spaces and nature's evocations.

For those seeking a novel that inspires creativity, this book is a treasure trove. The detailed character sketches and atmospheric descriptions transport readers into a world where the boundaries between reality and fiction blur. The narrative serves as a canvas, inviting readers to explore the intricacies of human emotion, the resilience of creativity and the eerie beauty of solitude. *The Cherry Robbers* is not just a gothic thriller; it is a journey into the depths of artistic expression, offering a lush and immersive experience that will resonate with readers who appreciate the intersection of dark tales and the creative spirit.

THE GOLDEN NOTEBOOK
by Doris Lessing

At the precipice of literary history, where brilliance and creativity intertwine, there exists *The Golden Notebook* by Doris Lessing – a beacon that beckons readers into a labyrinthine exploration of self and society. Imagine a canvas painted with the bold strokes of a woman's intellectual and emotional odyssey. Lessing, with her Nobel Prize-winning prowess, weaves a story that transcends time, and *The Golden Notebook* remains a feminist classic that continues to resonate with the pulsating heartbeats of contemporary feminists. At its core, the novel follows Anna Wulf, a writer grappling with the complexities of her existence through the medium of four distinct notebooks. Each notebook represents a facet of Anna's life: her African experiences, her political disillusionment, her creative endeavours and her personal struggles. As she navigates love, politics and the intricacies of her own psyche, Anna attempts to weave the threads of her fragmented identity into a cohesive narrative housed within a golden notebook.

This seminal work of contemporary fiction challenges conventional literary structures with its bold and innovative narrative technique. The interplay between Anna's traditional novel and her four notebooks offers readers a multifaceted exploration of identity, politics and creativity. Through Lessing's masterful storytelling, readers are invited to ponder profound questions about disillusionment, integration of the self and the elusive quest for fulfilment. The novel's enduring relevance is a testament to its ability to resonate with contemporary readers, offering insights into the human condition that transcend time and space.

Lessing's masterpiece not only serves as a feminist classic but also provokes introspection on the nature of storytelling and the transformative power of breakdowns. In her introduction, Lessing dismisses simplistic categorisations of the book, asserting that it is not strictly feminist or centred on finding the perfect partner. Instead, she suggests that the narrative embraces breakdowns as a path to healing, challenging readers to confront the messy and complex nature of human existence. *The Golden Notebook* has endured as a cornerstone of feminist literature, its exploration of women's aspirations aligning with the evolving perspectives of those who reject prescriptive notions of womanhood. *The Golden Notebook* confronts readers with the complexities of womanhood, identity and societal expectations. As Lessing herself aptly notes, it is the storyteller, the dream-maker and the myth-maker who represent humanity at its most creative – a sentiment that reverberates throughout the pages of this literary masterpiece.

HOW TO BE BOTH
by Ali Smith

This novel invites readers into an artistic labyrinth, a literary fresco where the brushstrokes of time create a mesmerising dance between past and present, fact and fiction. *How to Be Both* awaits you with open arms to welcome you into an exploration of art's boundless versatility. The book employs the fresco technique of painting to create a literary dance between genres, times, truths and fictions. In this fast-paced and genre-defying narrative, a Renaissance artist from the 1460s intersects with the child of the 1960s, weaving two tales of love and injustice into a singular yarn where time loses its linearity, structure becomes playful, the known becomes mysterious and the fictional becomes achingly real. The novel grants life's certainties a second chance, inviting readers into a realm of infinite possibilities.

At the heart of this creative marvel is the spirit of Virginia Woolf's *Orlando*, a mischievous, time-travelling, gender-crossing entity that transcends boundaries and defies conventional notions. Much like *Orlando*, *How to Be Both* reconciles opposites, blurring the lines between reality and fiction. The novel has received acclaim in literary circles for its clever storytelling, connecting the twentieth-century tale of loss and coping with the story of a female artist forced to navigate the complexities of life in fifteenth-century Italy.

Structured into two parts, the narrative unfolds the story of George (full name Georgia), a teenage girl grappling with the sudden loss of her mother. Intertwined with George's narrative is the tale of Francesco del Cossa, a real-life Renaissance artist. The connection between the two narratives is George's final trip with her mother to Italy to see a fresco painted by del Cossa. The novel presents an experimental twist, with half of the books printed with George's story first and the rest with the artist's story taking precedence. The prose, marked by stream-of-consciousness reflections, offers a vibrant and dynamic reading experience, seamlessly shifting between teenage thoughts and poetic, fragmented musings.

Ali Smith's *How to Be Both* stands as a playfully brilliant and genre-blurring work, shortlisted for the Booker Prize. It inspires excitement in recommending it to readers, navigating seamlessly through centuries, reflecting on art and grief, all while avoiding the pitfalls of its own postmodern intricacies. If you have an artistic side, and this book does not inspire you to pick up your paintbrush, I don't know what will.

EASY BEAUTY
by Chloé Cooper Jones

In the dimly-lit corners of a Brooklyn bar, Chloé Cooper Jones initiates a narrative that transcends the boundaries of her life as a disabled woman, a mother and an academic. Amidst the philosophical musings of her fellow doctoral students, who delve into the intricacies of clinical depression and launch into a discussion about her right to exist without seeking her input, Jones confronts the probing questions of belonging, worth and the elusive concepts of 'easy beauty' and 'difficult beauty'. As a philosophy professor, Jones infuses her memoir, *Easy Beauty*, with a magical essence, weaving famous philosophical theories into the fabric of her storytelling.

This memoir is a kaleidoscope of stories and vignettes that traverse Jones's life, each offering a fragment of the larger puzzle and another step towards understanding. From her poignant trip to Cambodia to encounters with profound art installations and the enchantment of a magic show in Prospect Park, each narrative thread exposes the rawness of her disability while simultaneously unravelling the fears, faults and inherent beauty that reside within us all. Jones eloquently captures the transformative power of beauty in the closing pages, reminding us that it enables us to be attentive to a world beyond our own self-absorption.

Throughout her journey, Cooper Jones discovers the profound joy of belonging and the pitfalls of self-imposed isolation to evade rejection. Her exploration of love, particularly a poignant moment where she questions her husband about enduring her constant search for answers, encapsulates the essence of her journey. His response reflects a profound truth – the commitment to being the person one would want to come home to. *Easy Beauty* emerges as a smart, fascinating, human and wise narrative, beckoning readers to explore the complexities of existence, belonging and the uncharted territories of self-discovery. It stands as a must-read for all humans seeking inspiration and wisdom.

YOUR FICTION READING LIST

Rosewater by Liv Little

explores the diverse and interconnected experiences of modern women,
offering up a critique on how we make and consume art

Wet Paint by Chloë Ashby

surges into the artistry of language, using poetry as a vibrant palette
to evoke emotions and explore the intricacies of relationships

Girl Reading by Katie Ward

weaves together multiple stories, exploring the transformative
power of art and portraiture across different historical periods

The Lady and the Unicorn by Tracy Chevalier

immerses readers in the vibrant world of medieval Paris, exploring
the creation of a renowned tapestry as a central artistic theme

What I Loved by Siri Hustvedt

weaves themes of art and friendship, exploring the impact
of the visual arts on personal relationships and the
human experience

Land of Milk and Honey by C. Pam Zhang

features artistry in its storytelling, capturing the essence of the Chinese
American experience through a powerful collection of stories

Death Valley by Melissa Broder
uses the art of poetry to explore the profound depths of desire and loss,
offering readers a visceral and emotionally charged experience

Reading Lolita in Tehran by Azar Nafisi
intertwines the transformative power of literature with the artistic
act of reading, illustrating the resilience of a group of women in the
face of political oppression

Watching Women & Girls by Danielle Pender
explores the art and representation of women, utilising
a collection of essays and stories to delve into the multifaceted ways
women are observed and portrayed, and creates a nuanced tapestry
that celebrates the diversity and resilience of women's experiences

The Poet by Louisa Reid
delves into the artistry of language and self-expression, as it follows the
journey of a young girl grappling with her identity through poetry

Sirens & Muses by Antonia Angress
weaves a narrative exploring the symbiotic relationship between
creativity and the feminine experience as well as the artistic
expressions of women and the transformative power of inspiration

YOUR NON-FICTION READING LIST

Big Magic by Elizabeth Gilbert
brings you a spirited exploration of creativity,
offering insights and inspiration to unleash the artistic
potential within each individual

You Could Make This Place Beautiful by Maggie Smith
uses artful language to contemplate the beauty and challenges
of life, creating a poignant reflection on the human experience

Strangers to Ourselves by Rachel Aviv
delves into the intricate narratives that shape our
understanding of self, utilising storytelling as an art form
to explore the complexities of the human mind

Stay True by Hua Hsu
delves into the connections between culture, identity and artistic
expression, exploring the ways in which individuals can maintain
authenticity in a complex world

The Flames by Sophie Haydock
utilises art as a lens to investigate historical mysteries and unsolved
crimes, offering a captivating exploration of the intersections
between art, storytelling and criminal investigations

The Artist's Way by Julia Cameron
offers readers a transformative guide that combines
art and spirituality, providing a roadmap to unlock
creativity and overcome creative blocks

The Multi-hyphen Method by Emma Gannon
explores the modern approach to work and creativity,
encouraging individuals to embrace their diverse skills
and passions in a changing professional landscape

You Are an Artist by Sarah Urist Green
explores the intersection of art and everyday life,
offering creative prompts and insights to inspire individuals
to express themselves artistically

Creative Confidence by Tom Kelley and David Kelley
offers readers a guide to unlocking one's creative
potential, emphasising the importance of confidence
and mindset in the creative process

Create Dangerously by Albert Camus
explores the role of the artist in society,
advocating for creative expression as a form of rebellion
against injustice and oppression

Bird by Bird by Anne Lamott
offers up a witty and insightful guide to the craft of
writing, blending humour and wisdom to inspire aspiring writers
to navigate the creative process

On Photography by Susan Sontag
examines the art of photography, delving into the cultural
implications and ethical considerations of capturing images

11.

escapism

The COVID-19 pandemic seems a lifetime ago, an impossible reality. I am not sure there was ever a time where we all, collectively, needed escapism more than during the pandemic years. It was a time where 35 per cent of the world was reading more, and 1 in 3 adults were reading more voraciously than ever. We needed an escape. Although times now seem less... unprecedented... (a word that forever and always will be reminiscent of the pandemic for me), we still require escapism from our everyday lives. Stressful jobs, screaming children, poor sleep, busy brains; there are so many reasons that connect us to a need to run in the direction of something new. Like meditation, reading is a mindful activity, and the books I will be recommending in this chapter will help you find a temporary, restorative escape to enter an entirely new world.

Opening the pages of a new book often feels like the beginning of a new journey. Similar to entering an enchanted realm, where the mundane constraints of reality yield to the limitless landscapes of the imagination. Whether you consider yourself a fantasy-loving reader or not, I hope to open your mind to exploring different worlds with my recommendations; be it fantastical worlds, utopian and dystopian. In this chapter, we delve into the transformative power of books as the ultimate escapism, exploring the therapeutic dimensions of bibliotherapy. As we traverse the diverse realms crafted by authors, we encounter the enchanting tapestry of genres such as magical realism, fantasy, mythical retellings and speculative fiction, each a portal to uncharted territories of the mind.

Magical realism, with its blend of the fantastical and the everyday, serves as a bridge between the real and the ethereal. Authors like Gabriel García Márquez or Isabel Allende weave tales where the extraordinary seamlessly intertwines with the mundane, offering readers a passport to worlds where the boundaries between reality and fantasy blur. This genre becomes a refuge, a literary sanctuary where readers can temporarily escape the constraints of their own existence and immerse themselves in the marvels of the extraordinary.

Fantasy, with its sprawling landscapes and fantastical creatures, beckons readers into worlds untethered by the rules of physics or the limitations of the ordinary. From J.R.R. Tolkien's Middle-earth to Juno Dawson's magical worlds, these imaginary realms provide solace and liberation, allowing readers to navigate realms where the impossible becomes plausible. Such escapades into the fantastical not only spark joy and wonder but also give the mind the freedom to soar beyond the confines of reality.

Mythical retellings, with their reinterpretations of age-old narratives, offer a fresh perspective on familiar tales. Authors like Madeline Miller or Neil Gaiman invite readers to reconsider the archetypal stories that have shaped cultural imaginations for centuries. These retellings become a therapeutic exploration, inviting readers to engage with timeless myths in ways that resonate with their own struggles, triumphs and metamorphoses.

Speculative fiction, in its myriad forms, propels readers into alternative realities, posing 'what if?' scenarios that challenge societal norms and envision divergent futures. Authors like Octavia Butler or Philip K. Dick craft narratives that act as both mirrors and windows, reflecting contemporary issues while also providing a lens into potential worlds. This genre invites readers to consider possibilities beyond the present, fostering a sense of agency and imagination crucial for navigating a complex world.

As we embark on this exploration of escapism through the lens of bibliotherapy, we unravel the intricate dance between fiction and reality. The cognitive and psychological benefits derived from the act of imagining new worlds, illustrating how these literary escapades can serve as a balm for the psyche, rejuvenating the spirit and expanding the horizons of the mind.

VIOLETA
by Isabel Allende

In a dance between reality and fantasy, Isabel Allende's *Violeta* unfolds as a mesmerising tapestry that stretches across a century, seamlessly blending the ordinary with the extraordinary. From the moment Violeta del Valle graces the world in 1920, a stormy backdrop sets the stage for a life that becomes a testament to resilience amidst the turbulence of the twentieth century. Allende weaves the threads of Violeta's life with a deft hand, navigating the ripples of the Great War and the Spanish Flu, both cosmic orchestrations that mark her entry into existence.

Violeta's narrative, painted with vivid strokes, unfolds as a letter – a poignant conversation with someone she cherishes above all. Through her words, we traverse an extraordinary journey punctuated by heartbreak, passionate affairs, the ebb and flow of fortunes, and the indomitable spirit that defines her. Set against the backdrop of the Great Depression, her family's retreat to a remote, untamed part of the country becomes a metaphorical pilgrimage, a space where Violeta matures, experiences first love and faces the profound transformations that life has to offer.

As Violeta navigates the contours of history, we witness her resilience against the fight for women's rights, the tumultuous rise and fall of tyrants, and the haunting shadows of not one but two pandemics. Isabel Allende, in her signature style, conjures a tale that is both fiercely inspiring and deeply emotional. Through the lens of magical realism, *Violeta* invites readers to escape into a world where history and imagination coalesce, creating a literary sanctuary that resonates with passion, determination and an indomitable sense of humour – attributes that carry Violeta through the tapestry of her turbulent yet vibrant lifetime.

HAMNET
by Maggie O'Farrell

In the tapestry of historical fiction, Maggie O'Farrell's *Hamnet* stands as a luminous thread, unravelling the enigmatic story behind one of Shakespeare's most revered plays. However, this narrative is distinctly Agnes's – a portrayal of Anne Hathaway – and it is her voice that echoes throughout the book. O'Farrell delicately sidesteps uttering Shakespeare's name directly, referring to him only as 'husband' or 'father'. It is Agnes, or Anne, who occupies the central stage, and the thematic heart of the novel pulsates with the complexities of motherhood – the joys, doubts, fears and sorrows that accompany raising children.

Within the nuanced portrayal of Agnes, readers encounter a woman transcending the conventional boundaries of her time. O'Farrell beautifully captures the essence of motherhood, intertwining Agnes's experiences with the constant questioning that accompanies parenting – am I doing enough? Could I do more? Starved for love as a child, Agnes forms an ethereal connection with nature, the animals and the forest becoming her companions. The narrative conjures images of a sprite-like figure, her ability to divine truths from the subtleties of others reminiscent of a mystical sensitivity.

The novel weaves seamlessly between Agnes's youth, courtship and pregnancies, and the sombre events of

1596 when tragedy befalls the Shakespearean household. O'Farrell artfully captures the universal fears of parenthood, the visceral and constant worry that something could go wrong. This theme is relatable to any parent who has experienced sleepless nights, acutely aware of the fragility of life. Through Agnes's story, *Hamnet* becomes not just a historical exploration but a deeply human narrative, delving into the emotional landscapes of love, loss and the enduring strength found within the realm of family.

YOUR FICTION READING LIST

The Left Hand of Darkness by Ursula K. Le Guin
explores themes of gender, identity and cultural differences on a distant planet

Great Circle by Maggie Shipstead
weaves together the stories of a daring female aviator in the early
twentieth century and a modern-day actress, exploring themes of
ambition, destiny and the pursuit of freedom

Circe by Madeline Miller
through a reimagining of Greek mythology this book offers a compelling
narrative centred around the enchantress Circe, exploring themes
of power, identity and resilience

The Book of Form and Emptiness by Ruth Ozeki
explores the themes of loss and finding solace through the lens of an
enchanting library of books, providing a unique perspective on grief

The Parable series by Octavia E. Butler
presents a thought-provoking exploration of religion,
survival and community in a dystopian future

Home Fire by Kamila Shamsie
tackles themes of love, sacrifice and the impact of political and cultural
tensions on a British Muslim family on the backdrop of a mythical retelling

The Mercies by Kiran Millwood Hargrave
weaves a historical narrative around the witch trials in seventeenth-century
Norway, exploring themes of resilience and resistance

1984 by George Orwell
delves into the consequences of totalitarianism, surveillance
and the manipulation of truth

The Handmaid's Tale by Margaret Atwood
explores a theocratic society where women are subjugated
and reproductive rights are controlled

Chain-Gang All-Stars by Nana Kwame Adjei-Brenyah
addresses social and cultural issues through a mix of humour
and poignant storytelling

Station Eleven by Emily St. John Mandel
interweaves multiple narratives to explore the interconnectedness
of lives amid a devastating pandemic

Zone One by Colson Whitehead
offers a unique take on the zombie apocalypse, blending horror
with social commentary on trauma and survival

The Rabbit Hutch by Tess Gunty
weaves a fantastical and eerie narrative set against the backdrop
of a crumbling American suburb

The Memory Police by Yōko Ogawa
explores themes of memory, loss and authoritarian control in a dystopian world

The Resisters by Gish Jen
addresses issues of technology, inequality and resistance,
providing a speculative perspective on the future

Version Control by Dexter Palmer
delves into the complexities of time travel
and its impact on relationships and society

The Warehouse by Rob Hart
critiques corporate power and surveillance in a dystopian setting,
exploring the consequences of unchecked capitalism

Blue Ticket by Sophie Mackintosh
explores themes of autonomy and societal expectations,
offering a speculative narrative on women's choices

The Dreamers by Karen Thompson Walker
delves into the mysterious and interconnected dreams of a community,
exploring themes of contagion and human connection

Brave New World by Aldous Huxley
critiques a society controlled by technology,
conditioning and the pursuit of pleasure

Her Majesty's Royal Coven by Juno Dawson
offers a whimsical exploration of magic and royalty,
blending fantasy elements with social commentary

The Companions by Katie M. Flynn
explores themes of artificial intelligence and human connection,
providing a speculative narrative on the future of technology

Her Body and Other Parties by Carmen Maria Machado
delves into feminist and speculative themes, offering a mix of horror and fantasy

Fen by Daisy Johnson
weaves a collection of atmospheric and darkly imaginative short stories,
exploring the uncanny and the mysterious

Rouge by Mona Awad
combines elements of satire and dark comedy, offering a narrative
that critiques societal expectations of beauty

Things We Say in the Dark by Kirsty Logan
explores the themes of horror and the supernatural, offering a
collection of unsettling and thought-provoking stories

**The Human Origins of Beatrice Porter
and Other Essential Ghosts** by Soraya Palmer
explores themes of identity and self-discovery set against the
backdrop of cultural mythology, providing a narrative that reflects
on the complexities of human existence

Love in Colour by Bolu Babalola
presents a collection of reimagined love stories from various
cultures, offering a fresh and diverse perspective on romance

Kindred by Octavia E. Butler
blends science-fiction with historical fiction, exploring themes
of slavery, agency and the complexities of time travel

12.

YOUR MIND

I t feels fitting to open this chapter with the immortal quote by Joseph Addison: 'Reading is to the mind what exercise is to the body.'

This is true, but I have experienced first-hand how, when your mind is in pain, it becomes less appealing to spend more time inside it. In this modern age, there are a million distractions we can choose which give us short-circuit dopamine hits – the inevitable doom-scroll on social media comes to mind. However, there really is nothing better for your mind in times of trouble than to open the pages of a book and lose yourself in the pages. Don't believe me? Picture yourself walking into a small, softly-lit bookshop off a busy road. As soon as the bell on the door announces your entrance and the door closes behind you, the noise and distraction of the bustling street is shut out. You are enveloped by the smell of fresh paperbacks, newborn ink. You look around at the bookshoppers enjoying the mutually agreed silence, disrupted only by whispers between browsers, sharing a joyful discovery from the stacks. I'm yet to find anyone who does not fall instantly under the spell of a bookshop upon entering, and I feel the same way about opening a book. The promise of being transported, the promise of calm and quiet, the promise of solace and connection – it is the same sensation of stepping into the promise of stories on a shelf, and when opening a book. These uniquely calming spaces in society, libraries alike, represent the calm the books they house can bring to the reader. Or take, for instance, a more modern example: Poems on the Underground. This is an initiative beloved by readers and non-readers alike. Whiteboards across the London Underground are regularly adorned with bespoke or beloved poetry, which we regularly photograph to commemorate, keep and typically share online with others. These words provide a simple escape, a fleeting moment of creativity that you'd be hard pressed to find anywhere else whilst in bustling and busy Underground stations. These are far more than 'oh-that's-nice' moments; they are a tiny and important beacon, offering a small escape from the stress of a commute – offering weary minds and stressed-out suit-clad train goers something mentally soothing. They are not trying to sell you something, there's no discreetly hidden call to action. Your challenge, should you choose to accept it, is to pause, read and enjoy.

As mentioned in the previous chapter, the biggest pause in our recent history was the pandemic. For so many of us, the years we spent inside, isolated and alone, were bookended quite literally with the escape into stories. The time we gained from having no commute, no social occasions, no obligations, sometimes no work, was filled with returning to our passions and comforts to find small meaningful joys. Speaking to my friends on Zoom and forming a book club was one of the few ways I was able to stay sane whilst shielding, and we all read voraciously. We chose books that featured sunny destinations, long embraces, short romances, all the things that felt fantastical at the time. We gushed over the passion and decadence of *Bridgerton* when it hit our pandemic TV screens, and we cried collectively for Connell and Marianne's enduring love in *Normal People* at a time where love in all its forms felt so distant. In short, as the famed quote from Mason Cooley goes: 'Reading gives us a place to go when we have to stay where we are.'[xix]

Historically, the perception of reading and its impact on the mind has shifted – from the passionate immersion in reading depicted in characters in *Madame Bovary* to the fearful reader in works such as *Northanger Abbey* and the tearful reader in *The Sorrows of Young Werther*. The nineteenth-century narrative reflects a struggle with separating life and literature, making characters hysterical. In contrast, now books are known to be a true balm to the soul, offering up myriad ways to distract and comfort us during anxious times. Even the first known self-help book, *Meditations*, by Marcus Aurelius, hits the nail on the head with its assessment of moving through anxious times with this quote: 'At dawn, when you have trouble getting out of bed, tell yourself: "I have to go to work – as a human being. What do I have to complain of, if I'm going to do what I was born for – the things I was brought into the world to do? Or is this what I was created for? To huddle under the blankets and stay warm?"'[xx] As literature evolved, the power of bibliotherapy emerged as an antidote to anxious minds. The act of reading offers a transformative escape, allowing readers to immerse themselves in alternate realities, explore different personas and embark on diverse adventures. This immersive engagement distances individuals from current concerns, providing a reprieve and contributing to better sleep and reduced cortisol levels.

You'll perhaps already be aware of the power of reading; what it can do for our brains as we age, what it can do to our mood and our sleep. Reading can reduce our ever-growing stress levels by up to 68 per cent, and has profound effects on reducing cognitive decline. A recent study showed that fiction readers live on average two years longer than non-readers. Basically, reading makes you live longer! When reading, it's proven that your heart rate slows and your eyes 'saccade' over the pages. This is the act of moving your eyes back and forth across the page, which creates a stress-reducing meditation state in your brain. It is close in practice to mindfulness and meditation. I myself have always seen a huge difference in the sleep I have after reading a couple of chapters, versus the broken sleep I fall victim to after scrolling on my phone before bed. Thinking back to the pandemic, it's absolutely no wonder that as well as giving us something to do, reading provided more comfort than binge-watching and (perhaps) banana bread. This is because when we read and use our imagination to envisage the story, we activate the same parts of our brain that are involved in experiencing real-life events and creating memories. In traditional practices of bibliotherapy, this is often the very reason a book is prescribed. The formal practice involves a bibliotherapist, a reader and a book that the bibliotherapist recommends based on the problems or stressors in the reader's life. The book(s) prescribed will then be in direct relation to the reader's own problems, so that they can identify with the characters in the book and reflect upon how the protagonist handled the situations they faced and moral dilemmas, and hope to apply what they had read to their own life. Being able to see how others deal with similar issues as yourself is one of the most compelling reasons for using bibliotherapy to find a specific book that speaks to you. When you identify with a fictional or non-fictional character, especially on an emotional level, you're able to see that there are others who are also navigating personal struggles. Reading a book and relating to its central characters is an experience not unlike making a new friend, and our brain processes that information in the same way. We learn from them, and are comforted by them, and they stay with us. This is not to say that books or indeed bibliotherapy are a replacement for traditional and proven scientific methods of treating mental ailments, but they help us to name and analyse our feelings, and tell us we are not alone.

I would invite you, reader, to choose a comfort book, series or album to help you through your hard times. Highlight your favourite quotes, earmark the pages that move you. If you are suffering yourself, clearly and sometimes beautifully articulated descriptions of mental anguish offer the understanding that we are never alone. Many have been there before us, and they can take the words from our heads and put them to page, and books can be in many ways a mirror to our own experience. If people have been there before, and survived it, so can you. Finding a comfort book that makes you feel this way will forever feel like sitting with an old friend, reading to you, and caring for you in your darkest moments.

SORROW AND BLISS
by Meg Mason

This is my comfort book. With a complex female protagonist figuring out life in messy, relatable ways, it is undeniably my desert island read. At a time in my life when it felt impossible to finish a page, Meg Mason's writing made me feel compelled to finish a book in just one weekend. This story breathed life into me, I felt intimately close to the characters, and I grieved their loss when the book was finished.

For anyone who has ever felt that their mental health is a burden, or that it deems them inadequate, this book and the story of Martha will make you feel less alone. I believe that the core purpose of any book is to keep us company, but when you find one as beautiful as this one, that feels close to your own experience, it is like finding a soulmate in page form. Meg Mason writes with reverence about how debilitating and life-altering undiagnosed mental issues can be, and Martha often feels as though she is a failure. She leaves her husband two days after his fortieth birthday and the story slaloms through her childhood and teenage years to the present day, where the messiness and uncontrollable misery began. In a narrative that drives so certainly towards the heartbreak of her divorce and life falling apart, it weaves together joy, humour and a true tapestry of what life presents to us, when you choose to notice it. A quote that has stayed with me, and encapsulates this story so entirely is: 'Everything is broken and messed up and completely fine. That is what life is. It's only the ratios that change, usually on their own.' Meg Mason concludes the book with a statement that 'This is a work of fiction. The nature and combination of medical symptoms described are not consistent with any actual mental illness.' It is true that this is entirely a work of fiction, but it is real, raw and honest. When looking for escapism in fiction, it would be very easy to turn away from the darkness. I would advise that in the case of books like this one, we should walk towards them, and be moved. Meg Mason beautifully captures a life of hurt and frustration, peppered like stars on a night sky with incredibly beautiful and meaningful memories. The darkness is vast, but the beauty is there.

THE BELL JAR
by Sylvia Plath

Once more, I have to include this book. In the haunting realm of Sylvia Plath's *The Bell Jar*, the crack-up of Esther Greenwood becomes a chilling exploration of the intricate landscapes of the mind. Plath's brilliance lies not only in crafting Esther as a character but in the uncanny ability to draw readers into the whirlwind of her unravelling psyche. The narrative unfolds like a mirror reflecting the internal dissonance many face, making Esther's descent into insanity a visceral and eerily relatable experience.

One cannot escape the omnipresent shadow of Plath's own struggles with mental health while traversing Esther's labyrinthine journey. Plath, like an omnipresent spectre, lingers within the musings of her protagonist, blurring the lines between fiction and the author's own reality. The poignant narrative is a testament to the raw authenticity Plath brings to the portrayal of Esther's thoughts, confusions and the gradual loss of momentum that propels her towards madness.

The Bell Jar serves as a literary tour de force, capturing the essence of Plath's poetic soul with precision. The language itself becomes a poignant medium, intricately weaving Esther's mood and her harrowing progression into madness. Plath's prose doesn't indulge in grandiosity or missteps; rather, it stands as both a testament and an almost melancholic farewell letter. In delving into Esther's psyche, Plath presents a narrative that transcends the boundaries of mere storytelling, offering readers a profound exploration of mental health that resonates beyond the pages.

HELLO BEAUTIFUL
by Ann Napolitano

In the emotionally charged landscape of Ann Napolitano's *Hello Beautiful*, the Padavano family story unfolds as a poignant exploration of love, loss and the complex tapestry of mental health. The novel delves into the lives of four sisters and the fractured young man, William, who becomes entwined with their destinies. Central to the narrative is the patriarch, Charlie Padavano, whose unconditional love, expressed through the endearing greeting 'Hello Beautiful', serves as a binding force for the family. However, as the story unfolds, fractures emerge, challenging the unity that once held them together.

Napolitano masterfully crafts characters that resonate with authenticity, mirroring the struggles and aspirations of real-life individuals. The sisters, akin to those in *Little Women*, navigate the delicate balance between individuality and familial closeness. The narrative extends beyond themes of independence, addressing the weight of familial expectations and the complexities of depression. As the characters grapple with mistakes made in the pursuit of saving their loved ones, the novel becomes a poignant reflection on the human condition.

Hello Beautiful is not merely a family drama; it's achingly beautiful in its portrayal of William Waters, a character shaped by a childhood marked by the absence of parental love. Napolitano traces his journey from finding solace in basketball to becoming an integral part of the Padavano family through his connection with Julia, the eldest sister. The novel explores the profound bonds of family, love and the impact of mental health on the choices one makes.

Napolitano's writing unfolds an extraordinarily moving narrative, weaving a gripping family drama around the resilient Padavano sisters. The story navigates the challenges they face as unity begins to fracture, tackling themes of love and loss. In the character of William, the author unearths a poignant exploration of mental health, emphasising the importance of self-discovery and acceptance amidst adversity. *Hello Beautiful* is more than a novel; it's a resonant portrayal of the human spirit's capacity to endure, grow and accept love despite the challenges life presents.

'THE YELLOW WALLPAPER'
by Charlotte Perkins Gilman

In the dim shadows of a colonial mansion, a woman grapples with the oppressive weight of both her physician husband's diagnosis and societal expectations in Charlotte Perkins Gilman's short story 'The Yellow Wallpaper'. Diagnosed with a 'temporary nervous depression' and a 'slight hysterical tendency' following childbirth, she is sequestered to a former nursery with barred windows and peeling yellow wallpaper. Forbidden from engaging in any productive activity, her only companions become the scratched floor and the haunting wallpaper.

As the days unfold, the woman's private journal becomes a canvas for her growing obsession with the peculiar pattern adorning the walls. In the moonlight, the wallpaper metamorphoses, revealing an unsettling figure within its design. Trapped in a confluence of societal restrictions and a room that embodies her stifled agency, the woman embarks on a quest to unravel the mystery within the wallpaper. However, this pursuit doesn't lead to clarity but plunges her into the abyss of madness.

'The Yellow Wallpaper' stands as a stark condemnation of patriarchal norms and the rampant misunderstanding and dismissal of women in late nineteenth-century society. Its chilling narrative serves as a historical marker, exposing the pervasive practice of dismissing women's mental health concerns as mere hysteria. Published in 1892, this landmark work unveils the societal constraints placed upon women, particularly in the realm of marriage and the perilous territory that follows the birth of their children. It echoes the struggle against the relegation of women's mental health to the shadows and serves as a poignant reminder of the enduring fight for recognition, understanding and agency in the face of oppressive norms.

WINTERING
by Katherine May

This novel is a beautifully crafted exploration of the intricate dance between the seasons of our lives. As readers traverse the pages, they embark on a journey through the metaphorical winters that Katherine May poignantly illuminates. The book's core theme revolves around the concept of 'wintering', a metaphorical state that mirrors nature's hibernation and invites readers to contemplate the periods of introspection, healing and renewal in their own lives.

One of the book's strengths, as voiced by numerous readers, lies in May's eloquent prose. Described as a comforting and introspective companion, the writing not only tells a personal narrative but also paints a broader picture of the collective human experience. May skilfully interweaves her own reflections with universal themes, creating a literary tapestry that resonates deeply with readers. The book becomes a sanctuary, offering solace and wisdom as it navigates the complexities of life's inevitable downturns.

Readers praise the accessibility of May's writing, appreciating how it strikes a delicate balance between literary depth and relatability. The narrative's exploration of the transformative power inherent in embracing life's challenges is a recurring theme in the reviews. By drawing parallels between the natural world and the human condition, *Wintering* becomes a guide for those seeking not just survival but a flourishing resilience in the face of adversity. It's a testament to the universality of the wintering experience and a celebration of the strength found in vulnerability, making it a timeless and invaluable addition to the literary landscape.

BROKEN
by Jenny Lawson

In Jenny Lawson's *Broken*, readers are welcomed into a world where humour serves as a lifeline amid the chaotic landscape of mental health struggles. There is such power in Lawson's distinctive ability to navigate the delicate balance between raw vulnerability and uproarious humour. The book, regarded by many as a triumph of candour, delves into the author's personal battles with mental health issues and their profound impact on her life.

Lawson's writing style, as lauded by reviewers, becomes a bridge that connects her readers to the often-tumultuous journey of self-discovery. The narrative not only tackles the challenges of mental health but also acts as a testament to the healing power of laughter. Many readers resonate with the poignant moments of reflection and the irreverent anecdotes that traverse the highs and lows of Lawson's experiences.

The literary merit of *Broken* lies not just in its comedic appeal but in its exploration of the complexities of human existence. Lawson's narrative craftsmanship transforms the seemingly broken fragments of her life into a mosaic of resilience. As readers navigate the highs and lows of her story, they find themselves not only entertained but also deeply moved by the raw authenticity that pervades the pages. *Broken* emerges as more than a memoir; it becomes an artful exploration of the human spirit, reminding us that, even in our brokenness, there is beauty, strength and the potential for healing.

YOUR FICTION READING LIST

How the One-armed Sister Sweeps Her House by Cherie Jones
crafts a powerful and evocative story, exploring themes of resilience, trauma and the interconnected lives of its characters

Big Swiss by Jen Beagin
weaves a quirky and compelling narrative, exploring themes of identity, love and the unexpected twists of life

Amazing Grace Adams by Fran Littlewood
tells a poignant story, delving into themes of grace, resilience and the transformative power of human connections

Ripe by Sarah Rose Etter
presents a unique and thought-provoking narrative, exploring unconventional themes and pushing the boundaries of storytelling

The Best Minds by Jonathan Rosen
explores the complexities of friendship, mental health and the human psyche, offering a compelling narrative that delves into the human experience

Evil Eye by Etaf Rum
crafts a suspenseful and thought-provoking tale, exploring themes of family, fate and the impact of cultural expectations

All My Rage by Sabaa Tahir
tells a powerful story, addressing themes of resilience,
identity and the search for justice

Kitchen and **Dead-End Memories** by Banana Yoshimoto
present a collection of poignant stories,
exploring the intricacies of life, love and memory

I Could Live Here Forever by Hanna Halperin
tells a reflective and introspective tale, exploring themes of belonging,
identity and the pursuit of happiness

The Travelling Cat Chronicles by Hiro Arikawa
shares a heartwarming and enchanting tale, exploring the bond
between a cat and its human companions

Strangers to Ourselves by Rachel Aviv
delves into the intricacies of the human mind and the
narratives that shape our understanding of mental health

Something Bad is Going to Happen by Jessie Stephens
crafts a narrative that explores the anticipation
and aftermath of challenging events

Yolk by Mary H.K. Choi
presents a nuanced and contemporary exploration of sisterhood
and identity, weaving a tale of resilience and self-discovery

An Emotion of Great Delight by Tahereh Mafi
crafts a compelling and emotional story,
exploring the complexities of human
emotions and resilience

Someday, Maybe by Onyi Nwabineli
offers a narrative that reflects on the possibilities
and uncertainties of the future, and the path forward from grief

Milk Teeth by Jessica Andrews
explores themes of identity, relationships and self-discovery,
presenting a contemporary narrative that resonates with readers

When We Were Friends by Holly Bourne
delves into the complexities of friendship and the evolution
of relationships, offering a relatable exploration of human connections

Acts of Desperation by Megan Nolan
presents a raw and unflinching portrayal of love
and desperation, exploring the darker aspects of relationships

After Leaving Mr Mackenzie by Jean Rhys
centres around Julia Martin, a woman navigating
the complexities of her relationships and life
as she struggles with financial
difficulties and societal expectations

***Everyone and Everything* by Nadine J. Cohen**
asks what makes us who we are and what
leads us onto ledges, in an intimate tale of a woman
coming back from the brink

***Good Morning, Midnight* by Jean Rhys**
follows Sasha Jansen, a woman adrift in 1930s Paris,
as she grapples with her past and present while
confronting loneliness and despair

***Hands* by Lauren Brown**
delves into the complexities of love, loss and self-discovery
as the protagonist, a young woman named Mia, grapples with
the impact of her mother's death and her own identity

***Freshwater* by Akwaeke Emezi**
explores identity and spirituality through the lens
of Ada, a young woman with multiple selves, as she
navigates her life and relationships

***Hamnet* by Maggie O'Farrell**
offers a beautiful escape into the world of Shakespeare's
spiritually gifted wife, Agnes, and the story of the domestic
life that happened in his absence

A Dutiful Boy by Mohsin Zaidi
chronicles the author's journey of self-discovery and acceptance
as a gay man from a conservative Muslim background

The Bread the Devil Knead by Lisa Allen-Agostini
delves into the complexities of love, identity and mental health
in the Caribbean, using evocative language to paint a vivid
portrait of a woman's journey

It's Kind of a Funny Story by Ned Vizzini
offers a poignant and humorous exploration of mental health,
blending elements of comedy and introspection

YOUR NON-FICTION READING LIST

A Manual for Being Human by Dr Sophie Mort
offers insights and guidance on navigating
the complexities of human existence

The Body Keeps the Score by Bessel van der Kolk
explores the intricate connections between the brain,
mind and body in the healing process of trauma

The Strength in Our Scars by Bianca Sparacino
explores resilience, healing and strength in
the face of life's challenges

Why Has Nobody Told Me This Before? by Dr Julie Smith
shares valuable and previously untold insights into mental
and physical well-being

My Mess Is a Bit of a Life by Georgia Pritchett
takes readers on a personal journey, sharing adventures
and insights related to anxiety and the messy business of coping

First, We Make the Beast Beautiful by Sarah Wilson
redefines the narrative around anxiety, offering a fresh
perspective and insights into the journey of living with anxiety

How I Learned to Live With Panic by Claire Eastham
shares her personal experiences and lessons
learned in coping with panic and daily anxiousness

Reasons to Stay Alive by Matt Haig
provides reasons for resilience and hope in the
face of mental health challenges

Hysterical by Pragya Agarwal
delves into the complexities of hysteria and its cultural
implications for women's mental health

Obsessive, Intrusive, Magical Thinking by Marianne Eloise
explores the intersection of neurodivergence, obsession and disorder

Camouflage by Sarah Bargiela
offers an engaging and accessible insight into the lives
and minds of autistic women, using real-life case studies

Enchantment by Katherine May
explores themes of enchantment and finding
magic in everyday life

Living While Black by Guilaine Kinouani
addresses the experiences of Black individuals and the
challenges they face navigating life and mental health

Maybe You Should Talk to Someone by Lori Gottlieb
shares insights from her experiences as a therapist
and patient and how we can seek help

It Didn't Start With You by Mark Wolynn
explores the intergenerational impact of trauma and its healing

Burnout by Emily and Amelia Nagoski
provides insights into managing stress and breaking the cycle of burnout

Inferno by Catherine Cho
shares a personal journey of mental health and recovery

Broken by Jenny Lawson
offers a humorous and candid exploration of mental health challenges

Laziness Does Not Exist by Devon Price
challenges societal notions of laziness and provides
a nuanced perspective on productivity

The Practice of Not Thinking by Ryunosuke Koike
explores mindfulness and the art of not overthinking

The Things You Can See Only When You Slow Down
by Haemin Sunim
guides readers to finding peace and mindfulness in the present moment,
offering insights and wisdom for a more fulfilling life

A Therapeutic Journey by Alain de Botton
explores the world of therapy, delving into the complexities of the human
mind and emotions, providing a thoughtful examination of our inner lives

The Perfectionist's Guide to Losing Control
by Katherine Morgan Schafler
offers a practical approach to overcoming perfectionism,
finding peace and embracing personal power

Notes on a Nervous Planet by Matt Haig
offers a thought-provoking exploration of modern life and its
impact on mental well-being, including practical advice for
navigating the challenges of our fast-paced world

Ten Times Calmer by Dr Kirren Schnack
provides a comprehensive guide to achieving a calmer and more
balanced life, with strategies and tools for managing stress
and improving mental well-being

A Beginner's Guide to Being Mental by Natasha Devon
offers an informative and accessible exploration of mental health,
providing insights and guidance for those looking to understand
and support their own well-being

The To-Do List and Other Debacles by Amy Jones
offers a humorous and relatable collection of essays that
explores the author's experiences with adulthood,
relationships and the challenges of everyday life

The Happiness Trap by Russ Harris
introduces readers to Acceptance and Commitment Therapy (ACT),
providing practical tools to break free from the happiness trap
and live a more meaningful life

Solve for Happy by Mo Gawdat
shares the author's journey to find joy and happiness
after the loss of his son, offering a unique perspective
on happiness and the principles needed to achieve it

**The Greatest Self-Help Book
(is the one written by you)** by Vex King
encourages readers to take charge of their lives
and become the authors of their own self-help journey,
fostering personal growth and empowerment

That Little Voice in Your Head by Mo Gawdat
explores the nature of the inner voice and provides insights into
mastering one's thoughts to achieve a more positive and fulfilling life

Stronger by Poorna Bell
chronicles the author's journey through grief and self-discovery,
offering inspiration and lessons on resilience and strength

The Colour of Madness by Samara Linton and Rianna Walcott
offers an anthology of poetry, prose and art that explores mental
health from the perspective of people of colour, challenging
stereotypes and fostering understanding

Poems for Stillness edited by Gaby Morgan
is a collection of poetry curated to provide moments of reflection and
stillness, offering solace and connection in times of quiet contemplation

Stress Less, Accomplish More by Emily Fletcher
introduces the practice of meditation and mindfulness to
reduce stress and enhance productivity, providing a practical
guide to incorporating these techniques into daily life

How to Feel Better by Cathy Rentzenbrink
provides a compassionate guide to navigating life's challenges,
drawing on the author's own experiences and offering practical
advice for finding comfort and healing

Choose Possibility by Sukhinder Singh Cassidy
explores the power of embracing possibility and reframing
challenges as opportunities for growth, providing insights into
creating a life of purpose and fulfilment

Toxic Childhood Stress by Dr Nadine Burke Harris
examines the impact of childhood stress on long-term health
and well-being, offering insights into mitigating its
effects and fostering resilience

How to Stay Sane by Philippa Perry
opens up a concise and accessible guide to maintaining mental
health, providing practical tips and insights for navigating the
complexities of modern life

Bigger Than Us by Fearne Cotton
explores the concept of self-love and offers guidance
on building resilience, fostering a positive mindset
and embracing one's unique journey

Jog On by Bella Mackie
explores the author's journey with running as a form of therapy,
highlighting the positive impact physical activity can have
on mental well-being

The Vagus Nerve Reset by Anna Ferguson
delves into the role of the vagus nerve in regulating the mind and body,
providing practical exercises and techniques to enhance well-being

No Such Thing as Normal by Bryony Gordon
challenges societal norms around mental health, sharing
personal stories and perspectives to break down stigma
and foster better understanding

The Book of Angst by Gwendoline Smith
is a humorous and relatable exploration of anxiety, providing
insights and coping strategies for managingthe challenges it presents

13.

grief & loss

At the most unexpected times, we find ourselves faced with grief and loss, cutting their way through the fabric of our lives. The profound ache that accompanies the departure of a loved one or the erosion of what once was can leave us adrift in a sea of complex emotions. It is within the pages of books, and the realm of bibliotherapy, that we often find refuge, understanding and a compassionate companion for the arduous journey through grief. Books offer embrace for wounded hearts.

In times of grief, books provide a sanctuary – a refuge that not only allows for a temporary escape from the weight of sorrow but also serves as a reflective mirror, resonating with the very essence of one's soul. The act of reading becomes a powerful antidote, offering solace and understanding when faced with the indescribable heaviness of loss. Contrary to the mindless scrolling online, which tends to amplify emotions, the immersive experience of delving into a book provides a more profound and empathetic connection. In the words of Roxane Gay, author of *Hunger*, the declaration, 'I am stronger than I am broken', encapsulates the resilience found within the pages, reinforcing the notion that literature, in its various forms, has the capacity to mend and strengthen the spirit in times of profound vulnerability.

This chapter unfolds at the intersection of literature and healing, exploring the poignant role books play in navigating the experience of grief. As grief has no prescribed path and each person's mourning journey is unique, books offer a diverse array of voices, perspectives and narratives that echo the multifaceted nature of loss. Through the empathy and wisdom encapsulated in written words, bibliotherapy extends a comforting hand to those grappling with the weight of grief, providing a space for reflection, solace and, ultimately, transformation.

Books become both mirrors and lanterns, reflecting our own experiences of loss and grief while casting light on the varied ways others have traversed similar terrain. Bibliotherapy, in this context, is not a cure for grief but a gentle guide, inviting readers to explore their emotions, share in the collective human experience of mourning, and find meaning amidst the shadows. Whether through memoirs that articulate the rawness of personal grief, fiction that explores the nuances of loss, or poetry that captures the inexpressible, literature becomes an indispensable companion in the grieving process.

THE YEAR OF MAGICAL THINKING
by Joan Didion

In the raw and electric honesty of Joan Didion's *The Year of Magical Thinking*, grief unfolds as a mysterious and unpredictable journey, a path illuminated by the piercing light of loss. The book begins with a poignant glimpse into Didion's shattered world, as she grapples with the abrupt and simultaneous illness of her daughter Quintana and the sudden death of her husband, John Gregory Dunne. Didion's writing becomes a cathartic journey, a struggle to comprehend the disorienting impact of death, illness and the unravelling of a partnership that spanned forty years.

The narrative is a testament to the unique nature of grief, defying any predetermined expectations. Didion's words resonate with the profound truth that grief is a place unknown until experienced, a place that fractures the fixed ideas about life, death, marriage and memory. Through the lens of her personal grieving process, Didion navigates the intricacies of loss, distinguishing the profound distinctions between losing a parent and losing a spouse. A poignant quote of her writing reads:

'Grief, when it comes, is nothing we expect it to be. Grief turns out to be a place none of us know until we reach it.'

The book captures the essence of grief as a non-linear, sporadic and unpredictable force. Didion eloquently expresses the struggle to keep the deceased alive in memory, the fear of forgetting and the realisation that, in order to move forward, one must ultimately let go. Anne Lamott's poignant words echo within the narrative, encapsulating the paradox of loss: 'It's like having a broken leg that never heals perfectly – that still hurts when the weather gets cold, but you learn to dance with the limp.'

Didion's narrative is a dance with the unpredictable, an acknowledgment that grief doesn't conform to a linear trajectory. The author's initial impulse to keep her husband's death a secret, hoping against hope for his return,

encapsulates the irrational and illogical nature of grief. *The Year of Magical Thinking* serves as a profound companion for those navigating the labyrinth of loss, offering solace, understanding and the reassurance that, in the midst of grief's chaos, one can learn to dance with the limp.

KITCHEN
by Banana Yoshimoto

Is there solace to be found in the act of cooking when confronted with the profound despondency that often accompanies loss? Delving into the culinary realm during times of grief, *Kitchen* raises questions about the therapeutic potential of preparing and sharing meals. In the intricate dance between life and loss, Banana Yoshimoto's *Kitchen* emerges as a poignant exploration of grief, resilience and the transformative power of connection. The narrative weaves a delicate tapestry around Mikage Sakurai, a young woman grappling with the recent loss of her grandmother – the final anchor to her familial past. This loss propels Mikage into the embrace of an unconventional makeshift family: Yuichi Tanabe and his mother, Eriko, who challenges societal norms as a transvestite running an all-night club.

Kitchen becomes a haven, a space where Mikage seeks solace and meaning amid the tumult of bereavement. The story unfolds with elegant simplicity, allowing the raw emotions of grief to permeate the narrative. Yoshimoto masterfully explores how personal tragedies shape our perceptions of life and death, depicting the intricate mechanisms that individuals employ to navigate the delicate balance between private sorrow and the demands of daily existence.

The kitchen, a seemingly mundane backdrop, evolves into a symbol of resilience and recovery. Mikage, deeply rooted in the culinary arts, discovers solace in the act of cooking. The shared meals become a communion of spirits, forging bonds and offering a glimpse of hope amid the shadows of loss. Yoshimoto's prose is a melodic cadence, inviting readers into Mikage's world with a graceful intimacy that resonates in the soul.

Through its companion story, the novella 'Moonlight Shadow', Yoshimoto continues her exploration of grief's profound impact on relationships. The tales, told through the eyes of young women navigating loss, showcase the author's gift for capturing the nuances of the human experience. *Kitchen* stands as a testament to the enduring power of kinship, offering readers a poignant reminder that, in the face of loss, new connections can blossom and kitchens can transform into sanctuaries of healing and hope.

TRANSCENDENT KINGDOM
by Yaa Gyasi

In the mesmerising tapestry of Yaa Gyasi's *Transcendent Kingdom* readers are enveloped into a narrative that transcends the boundaries of grief, addiction, and the complexities of familial relationships. The story unfurls as a woman grapples with the haunting spectres of a brother ensnared by addiction and a mother ensconced in the shadows of depression, all the while navigating her own ambitious pursuits. Gyasi intricately weaves a narrative that is deeply ruminative, profoundly moving and intensely searching, inviting readers on a journey through a thicket of ghosts that haunt both the characters' lives.

Transcendent Kingdom is a profound exploration of identity, loss, and the intricate dance between personal ambition and familial duty. The narrative goes beyond mere storytelling; it becomes an emotional odyssey that reverberates through the reader's soul. The book possesses the rare ability to rupture hearts and reshape perspectives simultaneously, leaving readers transformed, evolved, and more open-minded than before.

Alok Vaid-Menon aptly captures the essence of Gyasi's work, emphasising that it goes beyond merely addressing Blackness and gender. Instead, *Transcendent Kingdom* delves into the very essence of what it means to be alive – navigating the terrain of love, loss and longing. Gyasi's prose not only captures the nuances of individual struggles but also serves as a mirror reflecting the collective human experience. In a world pulsating with the rhythms of change, this novel emerges as a beacon, illuminating the interconnected threads of the human condition and inviting readers to confront the multifaceted layers of their own existence.

YOUR FICTION READING LIST

10 Minutes 38 Seconds in This Strange World
by Elif Shafak
follows the final moments in the life of Tequila Leila,
exploring her memories and the impact she has
left on those she encountered

Grief is the Thing with Feathers by Max Porter
explores grief, featuring a crow that serves
as a manifestation of mourning for a family in the wake of loss

Lessons in Chemistry by Bonnie Garmus
is a witty and empowering novel about a 1960s housewife turned
chemist who challenges societal expectations and pursues
her passion for science

Remarkably Bright Creatures by Shelby Van Pelt
weaves together the lives of two women,
exploring themes of identity, friendship and resilience

River Sing Me Home by Eleanor Shearer
offers a lyrical exploration of love, loss and the healing power
of nature in the context of the river

A House for Alice by Diana Evans
delves into the dynamics of a multicultural family, exploring themes
of love, loss and identity against the backdrop of London

You Made a Fool of Death with your Beauty
by Akwaeke Emezi
explores life after love and death, a tale of moving on
and learning to live with grief alongside new love

Tuesdays with Morrie and *The Five People you Meet in Heaven* by Mitch Albom
are two heartwarming and thought-provoking novels that delve
into life's important lessons, relationships and the impact
we have on others

Promise by Rachel Eliza Griffiths
examines themes of grief, resilience and the search for hope,
using powerful language to evoke emotional landscapes

YOUR NON-FICTION READING LIST

In Love by Amy Bloom
is a poignant love letter to Bloom's husband and a passionate
outpouring of grief, and reaffirms the power and value
of human relationships

Ti Amo by Hanne Ørstavik
follows a grieving widow as she recalls the many foreign trips
she enjoyed with her husband – but a particular one to
Venice sadly haunts her

Grief is Love by Marisa Renee Lee
explores what comes after death, and shows us that if we are
able to own and honour what we've lost, we can experience
a beautiful and joyful life in the midst of grief

The Worst Girl Gang Ever by Laura Buckingham
is the ultimate guide to recovery after miscarriage and
baby loss with guidance from experts

Heartsick by Jessie Stephens
is a deeply vulnerable look at grief and heartbreak in
a world that prefers to focus on the shiny things

The Long Goodbye by Meghan O'Rourke
is a beautiful memoir about her loss of a truly irreplaceable mother

When Breath Becomes Air by Paul Kalanithi
offers a poignant reflection on mortality as a neurosurgeon
is diagnosed with terminal cancer

Black Rainbow by Rachel Kelly
is the powerful first-person story of one woman's struggle
with depression and how she managed to recover
from it through the power of poetry

Moving On Doesn't Mean Letting Go by Gina Moffa
takes an honest look at how grief affects our lives,
offering a heartfelt, practical map through the dark

Crying in H Mart by Michelle Zauner
is a poignant memoir that reflects on grief, identity
and the author's relationship with her Korean heritage
through the lens of food and music

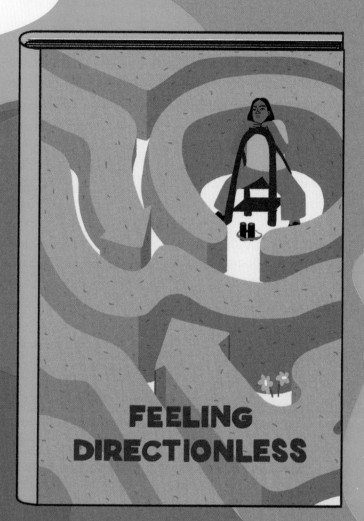

FEELING
DIRECTIONLESS

We all have moments where we just can't *even*. The world demands so much of us, and we only have so much to give. In the twists and turns of life's uncertainties, books are there for us. They offer solace, clarity and help through all the complexities we have to navigate.

This chapter delves into the profound intersection of literature and bibliotherapy, exploring their transformative potential in times of confusion, directionlessness and despair.

Books stand apart as a unique way to open our minds at times of confusion, offering up narratives, characters and situations which resonate with our own journeys. Books that feel like a dose of Big Sister Advice are the best remedy for times of complete indirection. The voices of writers and the characters they create become companions, mentors and confidants. It is in the pages of well-chosen novels, memoirs and self-help books that we often discover the mirrors reflecting our deepest quandaries and the much-needed light illuminating potential pathways forward.

I would wager that the feeling of complete directionlessness and hopelessness is one of the most isolating feelings there is. When life feels like each day blends into the next, that you are merely *existing* rather than living, it feels dehumanising. For me, it almost felt reductive that throughout my teenage life I had wished for my independence, and when I got it, there were many unexpected times when I just longed to be back at school, with the routine and guarantee of each day ahead. It seems that the more choices and paths we have available to us in life, the more befuddled we can become. If this does not apply to you, I'd like to meet you, because everyone I have ever met, no matter how professional, worldly or accomplished they appear, has confessed to feeling utterly hopeless at one stage or another. I've been told it's a right of passage, which was supposed to feel comforting, I believe, but any which way, we still have to get through these feelings alone, and carve out a direction – a sense of hope for ourselves.

A huge part of the quest for un-muddling these feelings is the quest for authenticity. I don't mind sharing that it took me a few years in therapy to understand what authenticity meant for me. On paper, I believed it looked like I had everything together. I had a thriving business, had just been featured on BBC's *Dragons' Den*, was in a long-term relationship, had many material things I never thought I'd have money to buy, and yet... There was a feeling of complete emptiness and confusion that consumed me every day. I could not say hand on heart that I knew who I was authentically, that I was living life truly for myself, to my own desires. Looking back, I know I was, like many of you may be as well, living a life I was told to want, a life I thought would make other people happy/impressed/(insert expectant emotion here). I have had conversations with friends whilst writing this book, this very chapter, when they feel terrified of changing the way their life looks but know that something *has* to change before they break. For me, my confusion and directionlessness led to destabilising every aspect of my life that served as a comfort zone, one by one. It felt horrid dismantling my life I had so carefully curated, but it wasn't for me. It did not make me happy. It was not authentic.

I turned to books, my therapist and trusted friends, and eventually I found my answers. I constructed a life that was terrifying at first; liberating myself from a toxic relationship, toxic friendships, away from the constant stress of running the business I thought I wanted, and instead I pursued authenticity. When you are reading this chapter and the books I recommend for you, I want you to ask that question of yourself. What is authenticity to me? Who am I, authentically? Who am I without a to-do list? These questions may seem scary; we spend our whole lives leading up to what will get us the Dream Job, told to follow the house-dog-marriage model, and I cannot blame a single person for feeling like this prescribed notion of what life *should* be leaves them a little… muddled. This chapter leans into authenticity, and shuns out the 'shoulds', and opens you up for MORE. (A note: The confusion and directionlessness I acted on forced me to change my life, radically. I never imagined I would be able to call myself a writer, to do the work I currently do full-time, which makes me unbelievably and wildly happy and fulfilled, and find love and friendships that make me glow brighter than I ever have. Change is good, and it's got your name on it.)

I would invite you, when reading the types of books I will recommend here, to take pen to paper (or pencil for those with delicate book etiquette sensibilities!) and write in the margins the findings you are taking from their writings. I have found myself doing so on numerous occasions, not knowing that this is part of the practice of expressive writing, which we touched on earlier in the book. Articulating your thoughts or responses to a text whilst reading it can be considered a form of journaling, and you may have already seen people on Bookstagram and Booktok taking to their books with highlighters, page tabs or other annotating accessories to document their journey through a story.

Whether grappling with existential questions, seeking direction in personal or professional pursuits, or confronting the void of hopelessness, literature emerges as a potent tool to illuminate the path ahead. Through a curated exploration of narratives that echo our own dilemmas, we can be guided towards newfound clarity, purpose and hope.

LETTER TO MY DAUGHTER
by Maya Angelou

With open arms, wisdom and warmth, Maya Angelou's *Letter to My Daughter* offers an embrace as a beacon of guidance, an intimate conversation with the myriad daughters she claims in the collective caress of her words. Dedicated to the daughter she never had but who she envisions all around her, the book transcends genres, seamlessly weaving elements of guidebook, memoir, poetry and sheer delight. It is, in essence, a testament to the enduring power of Angelou's voice, which resonates from the heart to touch the lives of the millions of women she considers her extended family.

The breadth of Angelou's offerings extends beyond the boundaries of race, religion, appearance or orientation. In her own words, she addresses a diverse tapestry of women, recognising the myriad ways in which the feminine spirit manifests itself. Through a series of essays, Angelou shares poignant life stories, imparts words of profound wisdom, and muses on topics that echo with relevance and meaning. Her style is not just literary; it's a reflection of her character – classy, disdainful of vulgarity, and a staunch advocate for humility and simplicity.

This literary gem is not just a book; it's a companion to cherish, savour, revisit and share. In moments of confusion or despair, *Letter to My Daughter* becomes a bedside refuge, offering solace through the timeless passages penned by a woman who exuded forward thinking, self-possession and an unwavering attitude of hopefulness and positivity. As Angelou herself once wrote, 'The ship of my life may or may not be sailing on calm and amiable seas. Stormy or sunny days, glorious or lonely nights, I maintain an attitude of gratitude. If I insist on being pessimistic, there is always tomorrow.' These words echo through the pages, a reminder that even in the stormiest seas of life, there is room for gratitude and the promise of a brighter tomorrow.

Within the pages of *Life of Pi*, the reader is thrust into the captivating narrative of Piscine Molitor Patel, a young Indian boy embarking on a perilous journey with his family aboard a freighter traversing the vast Pacific seas. Their cargo is not mere possessions but a menagerie of precious zoo animals bound for America for resettlement. The plot takes an unexpected turn one stormy night when the ship founders, leaving Pi adrift on a small lifeboat in the company of the surviving animals, including a massive Bengal tiger. As the vessel of hope sinks beneath the waves, Pi's extraordinary adventure begins – a tale of resilience, survival and an unlikely companionship that defies the conventions of the animal kingdom.

In the vast ocean of literature, *Life of Pi* by Yann Martel stands as a transformative journey that defies expectations, leaving readers not only moved but also contemplating the essence of life, faith and the art of storytelling. Much like the deceptive simplicity of a magician's act, Martel weaves a tale that lingers in the reader's mind, beckoning them to reassess the narrative and its underlying truths. It is an exploration of the extraordinary within the ordinary, where the story, much like life itself, takes unexpected turns and the journey proves more profound than the destination.

Stranded in the middle of the boundless seas, Pi must confront the harsh realities of survival with scant resources and the daunting presence of one of the world's deadliest predators. The narrative unfolds as a testament to the human spirit's capacity to endure, adapt and find solace in the most unimaginable of alliances. Through months of isolation and uncertainty, Pi's story becomes an exploration of the thin line between fear and courage, vulnerability and strength. The struggle for survival becomes a metaphorical journey, inviting readers to reflect on their own battles with the storms of life.

As Pi grapples with the challenges of his seafaring odyssey, Yann Martel intricately weaves a tale that transcends the mere physicality of survival. *Life of Pi* becomes a philosophical exploration, prompting readers to question the narratives they construct in the face of adversity and the transformative power of storytelling itself. The blurb's reimagining emphasises the rich layers of the novel – a narrative that sails beyond the traditional boundaries of adventure, inviting readers to embark on a voyage of self-discovery, resilience and the unexpected connections that shape the human experience.

Marilynne Robinson's *Gilead* unfolds as a luminous thread, weaving together the intricate patterns of life, love and the quiet contemplation of the human spirit. As John Ames, a septuagenarian minister whose heart is faltering, endeavours to leave a legacy for his young son, the narrative becomes a vessel of profound wisdom and introspection. The act of writing a letter to his seven-year-old child transforms into a testament to the inexhaustible resilience of the human soul in the face of life's uncertainties and imminent mortality.

Robinson's prose, akin to a gentle stream, flows through the narrative, infusing it with a quiet grace that belies the weighty themes it carries. *Gilead* is more than a novel; it is a profound meditation on the nuances of existence, a celebration of the interconnectedness between the inner and outer realms of human experience. In the heart of the book, the reader encounters life-affirming wisdom generously dispensed by John Ames. The novel becomes a sanctuary, offering solace to those grappling with confusion, hopelessness or the need for direction.

The beauty of *Gilead* lies in its capacity to resonate as a balm for the weary heart. The soft, loving voice of John Ames becomes an intimate guide, inviting readers into the inner recesses of his mind and heart. The narrative's exploration of openness, kindness and the enduring human spirit unfolds as a poignant reminder of the potential for grace and redemption, even in the face of perceived disconnection. At its core, *Gilead* is not just a literary work; it is a compassionate embrace, a blessing that extends beyond the characters on the pages to touch the very essence of those who embark on this literary journey.

THE FORTY RULES OF LOVE
by Elif Shafak

Embark on a journey through time and souls with Elif Shafak's *The Forty Rules of Love*, a literary tapestry interwoven with the parallel lives of Rumi and Shams of Tabriz in the thirteenth century, alongside the contemporary narratives of Ella, a Massachusetts housewife, and Aziz Z. Zahara, the peripatetic author of the book she edits. Shafak's narrative prowess shines as she tells Rumi and Shams' story through the perspectives of those around them, weaving a rich tapestry of voices – from Rumi's diverse sons to a leper outside the mosque, a brothel-bound prostitute, Rumi's wife, and more. The female characters, in particular, take centre stage as they grapple with applying Shams' forty rules to their lives, discovering that these rules, though profound, aren't always a seamless fit.

In this lyrical masterpiece, Shafak unfolds two narratives – one set in the thirteenth century, portraying Rumi's encounter with Shams, and the other contemporary, following Ella's journey with Aziz Z. Zahara. Through these entwined stories, Shafak brings to life Rumi's timeless message of love, inviting readers to contemplate the forty rules that resonate across centuries. The novel serves as a poignant reminder that love, in all its forms, has the power to transcend time and transform lives.

Among the forty rules that linger in the reader's mind, one stands out: 'Fourteenth Rule: Try not to resist the changes that come your way. Instead let life live through you. And do not worry that your life is turning upside down. How do you know that the side you are used to is better than the one to come?' This rule encapsulates the essence of the novel – a call to embrace change, uncertainty and the unexpected twists that life unfurls.

In a world where love and friendship are often tales of unexpected transformation, Shafak offers profound insight: 'Every true love and friendship is a story of unexpected transformation. If we are the same person before and after we loved, that means we haven't loved enough.' Through these words, the author invites readers to delve into the intricate web of human connections, urging them to explore the transformative power of love. *The Forty Rules of Love* is a literary masterpiece that not only captivates with its lyrical prose but also imparts timeless wisdom to those navigating the complexities of life and love.

YOUR FICTION READING LIST

The Alchemist by Paulo Coelho
is a beautiful parable about learning to listen to your heart, read the omens
strewn along life's path and, above all, follow your dreams

Catcher in the Rye by J.D. Salinger
is an all-time classic in coming-of-age literature – an elegy to teenage
alienation, capturing the deeply human need for connection

Odes to Common Things by Pablo Neruda
brings a beautiful collection of 25 odes – in both English and Spanish –
from one of greatest poets of the twentieth century. Each poem in this
collection is accompanied by a pair of exquisite pencil drawings

The House in the Cerulean Sea by T.J. Klune
is a modern fairy tale about understanding your true nature
and learning what you love and will protect

A Psalm for the Wild Built by Becky Chambers
is a wonderfully calm and philosphical novel that touches
on human nature, friendship and the need for purpose in
a world different, but familiar, to our own

Remarkably Bright Creatures by Shelby Van Pelt
traces a widow's unlikely connection with a giant Pacific octopus in an
exploration of friendship, reckoning and hope

On the Come Up by Angie Thomas
is the story of sixteen-year-old Brit, an aspiring rapper, daughter of a
murdered father, living in a tough American neighbourhood

Convenience Store Woman by Sayaka Murata
is a deadpan Japanese tale of an oddball shop
assistant who possesses a strange beauty

The Humans by Matt Haig
is a funny, compulsively readable novel about alien
abduction and mathematics

YOUR NON-FICTION READING LIST

A New Earth by Eckhart Tolle
explores the concept of mindfulness and the
transformative power of living in the present moment

The Book of Hope by Douglas Abrams and Jane Goodall
offers insights and perspectives on finding hope
and purpose in challenging times

For Small Creatures Such as We by Sasha Sagan
offers a thoughtful exploration of rituals and traditions
that bring meaning to our lives, rooted in the author's
experiences and reflections

Becoming Wise by Krista Tippett
explores wisdom, spirituality and the art of living a meaningful life

Becoming by Michelle Obama
traces the life of the former First Lady, in a deeply personal memoir that
explores her journey, challenges and the evolution of her identity

You Are Here (For Now) by Adam J. Kurtz
offers a creative and humorous guidebook that encourages
self-reflection and finding one's way in the world

Hope in the Dark by Rebecca Solnit
explores themes of hope and activism, drawing on
untold histories and envisioning positive
possibilities for the future

Wilding by Isabella Tree
narrates the author's experiences of transforming
a traditional farm into a rewilded landscape,
exploring the positive impact on biodiversity

How Dare the Sun Rise by Sandra Uwiringiyimana
recounts the author's journey as a survivor of war
and her advocacy for refugees

A Paradise Built in Hell by Rebecca Solnit
examines the surprising and inspiring communities
that emerge in the aftermath of disasters, challenging
conventional views of human behaviour

Ladder to the Light by Steven Charleston
brings together a collection of meditations offering wisdom
and hope from an Indigenous perspective

Tomorrow Will Be Different by Sarah McBride
shares the author's personal journey
as a transgender advocate and political leader

Where to Begin by Cleo Wade
encourages readers to tap into their power for
positive change in the world

Hope Is a Verb by Emily Ehlers
provides practical steps for cultivating radical
optimism in the face of challenges

REFERENCES

'Adult Bibliotherapy: Books Help to Heal', *Journal of Reading*, vol.23, no.1, October 1979, pp.33–35 (International Literacy Association)

Cacchioli, Serena 'The Healing Power of Books: The Novel Cure as a Culturally Tailored Literary Experiment', *Reading Today*, 2018, pp.145–56 (UCL Press)

Canavan, Tony 'The Power of Words: Bibliotherapy and Better Mental Health', Books Ireland, no.354, March/April 2014, pp.18–19, (Wordwell Ltd.)

Gubert, Betty K. 'Sadie Peterson Delaney: Pioneer Bibliotherapist', *American Libraries*, vol.24, no.2, February 1993, pp.124–30 (American Library Association)

Miller, Jesse 'Medicines of the Soul', *Mosaic: An Interdisciplinary Critical Journal*, vol.51, no.2, June 2018, pp.17–34 (University of Manitoba)

Neville, Patricia 'The Reading Cure?: Bibliotherapy, Healthy Reading Schemes and the Treatment of Mental Illness in Ireland', *International Review of Modern Sociology*, vol.36, no.2, 2010, pp. 221–44, (International Journals)

ENDNOTES

INTRODUCTION

i   Alan Bennett, *The History Boys* (Faber & Faber, 2004)

ii   Judith Butler, 'What Value do the Humanities Have?' McGill University speech, May 30, 2013

iii   *The Atlantic Monthly*, 'A Literary Clinic' (1916)

iv   George Eliot, From '*The Natural History of German Life*' Reprinted from *The Westminster Review*, vol.66, July 1856, pp.28–44

v   James Baldwin, *Giovanni's Room* (Penguin Classics, 2007)

vi   George R.R. Martin, *A Dance with Dragons* (Harper Voyager, 2011)

vii   Oscar Wilde, *The Decay of Lying: And Other Essays* (Penguin Classics, 2010)

viii   Annie Dillard, *The Living: A Novel* (Harper Perennial, 2013)

ix   Stephen King, *On Writing: A Memoir of the Craft* (Hodder, 2012)

x   Abraham Lincoln, *The Wit & Wisdom of Abraham Lincoln: A Treasury of Quotations, Anecdotes, and Observations* (Gramercy Books, 1999)

xi   René Descartes, *Discourse on Method and Meditations on First Philosophy* (Fourth Edition). Translated by Donald A. Cress (Hackett Publishing, 1998)

xii   Arthur Lerner, *The American Journal of Nursing* vol.78, no.8, 1986, pp.1336-8

xiii   Adrienne Rich, 'Someone Is Writing a Poem' from *What Is Found There: Notebooks on Poetry and Politics* (W. W. Norton & Co. 1993)

xiv   Frampton D.R. 'Restoring Creativity to the Dying Patient', *British Medical Journal*, vol.93, 1986, pp.1593-5

WHEN ADULTING BEGINS

xv   Julia Cameron, *The Artist's Way: A Course in Discovering and Recovering Your Creative Self* (Pan Books, 1995)

FIRST LOVES & GREAT LOVES

xvi   Jane Austen, *Mansfield Park* (Penguin Classics, 2003)

LGBTQIA+ IDENTITY

xvii   Scarlett Curtis, www.womensprizeforfiction.co.uk/features/tag/scarlett-curtis/feed

CREATIVITY & INSPIRATION

xviii   Sylvia Plath, *The Unabridged Journals of Sylvia Plath* (Anchor Books, 2000)

YOUR MIND

xix   Joseph Addison, *Addison's Essays from the Spectator* (Adamant Media Corporation, 2001)

xx   Mason Cooley, *Aphorisms of the All-Too-Human* (Ragged Edge Press, 2000)

xxi   Marcus Aurelius, *Meditations* (Penguin Classics, 2006)

Molly Masters is a writer, podcaster, director and CEO of Aphra, and CEO of Bookshop Limited. Molly's experience in bookselling and book subscriptions brought her to beginning the podcast The Chapters, now Book Therapy, to pair book recommendations to aid dilemmas sent in by listeners. Throughout writing *Bibliotherapy*, she has also been training officially as a bibliotherapist.